A Letter Is Better!

The Art of Thank You

A Letter Is Better!

The Art of Thank You

ERICA GERARD DI BONA

SPARK Publications
Charlotte, North Carolina

A Letter Is Better!
The Art of Thank You
Erica Gerard Di Bona

Designed, produced, and published by
SPARK Publications
SPARKpublications.com
Charlotte, North Carolina

Cover, back cover, section openers, and author portrait:
Steve Cohn Photography/SteveCohnPhotography.com

Pull Quote Stamp Images: oleskalashnik/shutterstock.com

Typewriter
Silver and gold design created by Helmut Schulze of Rees Electronics/ReesElectronics.com

Printed in the United States of America

Hardback, October 2025, ISBN: 978-1-953555-86-1
Paperback, October 2025, ISBN: 978-1-953555-91-5
Library of Congress Control Number: 2025904585

To protect privacy, many original notes and letters have had mailing addresses and other contact information removed.

Dedication

I dedicate this to Granddaddy Al,
who happily shared his pleasure of
weekly correspondence with me.

In Their Own Words

THANK YOU notes could very well be the secret to my success and what distinguishes me from the "others" ...

It's when they're least expected ... and an expression of "thanks" for the small things means the most and is long remembered.

Write a note, let your heart do the composition, and you'll long be remembered as one in a thousand ... just like Erica, she literally wrote the book!

Bruce Meyer
Founding Chairman,
Petersen Automotive Museum

Gratitude is one of the most important parts of happiness and making sure we show our heartfelt gratitude is important for the recipient as well as the giver.

Erica has shown us how to make a real difference in expressing genuine appreciation which goes above a simple acknowledgement. We both agree that thank you notes are a lasting and more meaningful way to say we care about our relationships and acknowledging the thoughtfulness of the giver.

Writing personal thank you notes has served me well in all aspects of my life including philanthropy for stewardship of committee members and donors alike.

Christine Udvar-Hazy
Co-Founder, National Air & Space Museum; Co-Chair,
The Smithsonian Campaign for Our Shared Future

Every year for my birthday Erica has sent me my Horoscope.
I look forward to it.
I appreciate it
and
I finally know what is happening in my life.
Erica is my thoughtful and caring friend.
How lucky am I.

Henry Winkler
Actor, Producer,
Director, and Author

Whenever I go to my mailbox and find a personalized typed envelope from Erica Gerard Di Bona, I always get excited because I know inside will be one of her gems, a beautifully typed letter or note that sets her message apart from any other mail I may receive.

Erica's letters are exceptional because they are a throwback to an earlier time when people made each message special and noteworthy. She is that rare individual whose humanity radiates forth in everything she chooses to do.

Out of the blue, she can send a thank you note for the slightest courtesy you may have shown or dispatch a congratulatory missive about some recent accolade you may have gotten. She notices everything, forgets nothing and executes it all with style and grace.

In summary, I am a big fan because she does something almost no one else does these days. She sends the classiest, most elegant typed letters that brighten our mailboxes and bring joy to our lives. They are a thing of Beauty, making Erica the real deal.

Charles Floyd Johnson
Television and Film Producer

I know we have all received beautiful gifts. Erica's "thank you" notes are like an exquisitely wrapped gift with a wonderful present inside. I have taken great delight in collecting and carefully filing them for safekeeping—they are amazing!

The art of writing a "thank you" note is alive and well with Erica Gerard Di Bona!

Donelle Dadigan
Founder, Hollywood Museum

Erica's nostalgic style of communicating is an endearing superpower. Her grace, wit, and honesty have irresistible influence. And it is FUN. Her successful lifestyle and details about why and how to type letters are generously explained in this how-to memoir. Written as your personal mentor, everyone can benefit from trying this simple process of typing letters of gratitude.

Louise A. Marler
Typewriter Artist, L.A. Marler

Erica Di Bona is a supreme love goddess, spreading her magic and goodness with heartfelt, snail mail letters. Read her stories and they will inspire you to get some pretty paper. Then follow her instructions, and you too can spread the love. Watch how what goes around will come back around.

Annie Sprinkle
Author of *Assuming the Ecosexual Position— the Earth as Lover*

Several times a year for the past decade or so, I receive a decidedly hand-crafted letter in the mail that makes my day. I know immediately from the typed addresses, the specifics of the stationery (often from a far-away hotel), and carefully selected stamp, that I am in for a treat from my friend Erica. Sometimes it is a thoughtful thank you note, sometimes a note of congratulation for something that I have done in the world that Erica thinks deserves acknowledgement or celebration, but most often it includes an article clipped from a (actual) paper or magazine, along with a typed note explaining why she sent it to me, and her thoughts on the piece. These letters are usually short and concise, but always so full of thoughtfulness, intention and kindness that they have become an important and cherished addition to my life.

Adam Silverman
Los Angeles-based Artist

Erica Di Bona is the consummate "thank you" note writer!

I have been receiving her "thank you" notes for many years—each one is truly a work of literary art!

Erica's thank-you letter radiates warmth, thoughtfulness, and impeccable grace, turning a simple expression of gratitude into an art form. Her words flow with effortless civility, each sentence carefully chosen to honor both sentiment and sincerity. The beauty of her letter lies in its delicate balance—neither overly formal nor casual, but perfectly poised in the realm of genuine appreciation. Through her refined yet heartfelt phrasing, she transforms gratitude into an experience, leaving the recipient feeling truly seen and valued. It is a letter not merely read but felt, embodying the elegance of gratitude at its most profound.

Michael Spalter
Chair, Rhode Island School of Design, 2009-2023

A thank-you letter from Erica is like receiving a bejeweled gift box that, when opened, immediately amplifies joy and connection. Such amplifications are essential, as they affirm that we are not only seen but appreciated and valued. And so, her letters are themselves a gift for which I am perpetually grateful. I treasure my stack of gleaming Di Bona notes and am reminded, when I glance at them, that there is still sweetness, kindness, thoughtfulness, humility, and appreciation between many of us. That, too, is a gift.

Crystal Williams
18th President, Rhode Island School of Design, Award-Winning Poet

---

WHAT IT FEELS LIKE TO RECEIVE A PERSONAL NOTE FROM YOU

It's always a wonderful moment of surprise and anticipation to receive one of Erica's typewritten envelopes knowing that inside is a treasure—a considerate typewritten note just for us—unlike anything many people have ever seen!

In fact, a communication from you, Erica, is not just a note; it's an experience that stands out like nothing else we've ever pulled from our mailbox!

Your letters have reminded us of the power of a simple, heartfelt message—uniquely presented. It lingers long after it reaches its addressee—for who in the world would discard a hand-typed and artful communication like yours? One can only imagine that many of your messages—typed with love—have been framed and adorn the walls of homes and offices.

A special typewritten note from Erica Di Bona—is a Godwink in an envelope!

SQuire Rushnell & Louise DuArt Rushnell
Authors, Godwink Book Series

Expressing gratitude is all the more powerful when commemorated in a timely, crafted note—typewritten messages require intention and care. The message rises above transience. It reflects commitment. People often respond to thank you notes that are typewritten.

Erica Gerard Di Bona has produced a book that opens my heart, connects me to others ... builds belonging. Thank you for the commitment you took to write this gently and importantly persuasive book, Erica!

Pamela Rogow
Owner, W.P.M. Typewriter Shop, Philadelphia

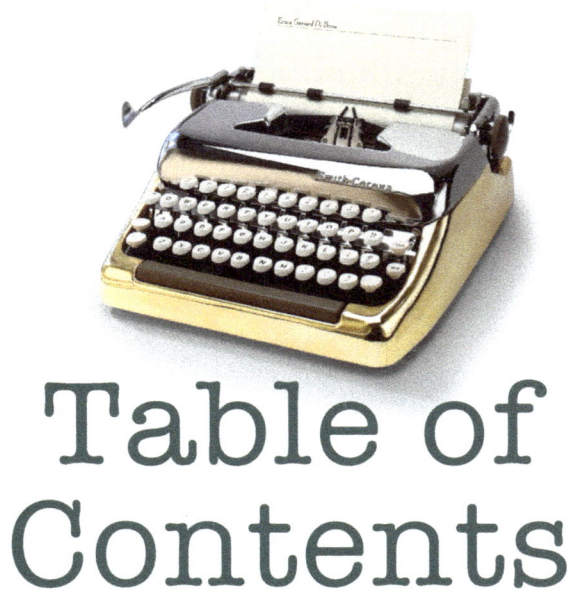

Table of Contents

Foreword

April 25, 2025

To Whom It May Concern,

This is a letter typed on an iPad about receiving letters typed on a variety of typewriters from the brilliant, convivial, effervescent woman of letters, Erica Gerard Di Bona.

I have known Erica for close to twenty years now, and by way of introduction, I originally received a typewritten letter from her, which was soon followed by a scanned version of the same delivered via email. Talk about a blend of old school and new school! And during these last two decades in which our paths have crossed both personally and professionally, I have been the lucky recipient of many more such letters and follow-up emails. The subjects have ranged from a clipping about a trade article on a new television series we deployed to the world to a quick thought about how to support our shared alma mater. Or even just a congratulatory note about a child's graduation.

Always timely. Always typed on real paper with a real typewriter and dropped in the mail. And, for good measure, an electronic version to cap it off.

Long before I knew of Erica's love of typewriters, her unique style of sending real letters made an impression. It speaks to effort, thought, and the investment of time. It's not a text, voicemail, or hastily constructed email. Erica has to compose a message, navigate the possibility of mistyping and making corrections (maybe I am projecting here), find an envelope, seal it, stamp it, and get it into the U.S. Mail system. In an increasingly efficiency-focused communications environment, this is tantamount to handcrafting furniture as opposed to swinging by IKEA.

Adding to Erica's now legendary stature as a preservationist of the centuries-old method of tangible correspondence is her equally epic positive attitude and joyous approach to life. Erica is a great friend, spouse, professional, and teammate. She lights up every room she is in, and that same energy pops off the page of her beautiful letters.

My own experience with typewriters dates back to the early 1970s, when I would watch my grandmother, who had worked for years as a church secretary, blazing through her own letters at eighty words per minute with a standard Remington machine of dubious provenance and the stickiest keys ever known. In an effort to emulate her skills, I would load my own piece of paper and, using one finger, try to manipulate the keys into something readable. Like many explorations in youth, it was quickly supplanted with something more interesting, like throwing rocks at squirrels or digging up earthworms for fish bait, and I didn't think much about how I might have to actually learn to type myself. But many years later, as a sophomore in high school, an intro to typing class was a requirement, and I—along with thirty other classmates—reluctantly sat down in Mrs. Barnard's class with a sea of IBM Selectric II machines. Like conventional steering gave way to power steering in automobiles, the speed of the Selectrics was amazing. But the frequency of typing mistakes increased proportionally with that speed. I never worked harder in any class in high school to try and get that A, and it all came down to typing multiple perfect documents at a minimum of sixty words per minute. I must have squeaked by and hoped that I would never have to use these typing skills ever again. The poor evaluators who read my horrific handwritten versions of the AP English, U.S. History, and other exams must have wished that typed responses were OK way back in the mid-1980s, but it was not to be.

The one purchase my parents gifted me with before going off to college was an electric typewriter. Mind you, it was not an IBM Selectric II but more likely a Brother or other brand. I lugged that into my dorm room, along with a futon and my few CDs, and declared myself an emancipated adult.

I recall getting through a couple of papers using the typewriter before someone down the hall mentioned the existence of a new "Apple Computer". A magical device that could let you type on a screen, make corrections before anything was expressed in print, and could actually save your work. When I saw it in action, it was as if a modern miracle had occurred before my eyes. I quickly mastered the art of trading meal tickets and other premium goods for "Mac Time", and gave away my typewriter.

And skipping ahead a few years to my first job in television, my ability to type and edit quickly ensured a long-running job as an assistant and eventual producer on a successful television series. Thankfully, I have been employed and have kept typing ever since, but absent that high school typing class, I would be nowhere.

So, it is with even more appreciation and affection that I continue to receive and cherish the thoughtful and cheerful letters from Erica. It's both a reminder of the distant and not-so-distant past, and a connection to my grandmother and mother, both gifted typists.

Erica's special brilliance around honoring the old and embracing the new, is just one of the ways she shares herself with the world, and all of us are better off for it.

Kevin Beggs
Chair of the Lionsgate Television Group
and Lionsgate Chief Content Integration Officer
San Marino, CA

Introduction

I grew up reading advice columnists like Dear Abby and Ann Landers (who were competitive twins, I later discovered). I always thought about how cool it would be to help people solve problems and make light out of darkness.

I landed in the entertainment field, which lacked courtesy for the most part, so I made it my mission to change the dynamic and took it upon myself to issue thanks, encouragement, and kindness to those I knew and people who randomly came into my life, even just once—my own version of "Dear Erica." Now, decades later, despite thinking I wouldn't have firsthand knowledge concerning *anything* to offer advice about, here I am, about to share my deep connection and commitment to what sustained me all those years through good times and bad: writing "Thank You" letters, including a few to encourage myself.

Letter writing is also an antidote—my way of delivering a ray of light to offset the cruelty around us. My father was a Holocaust survivor, and I learned early on about that horrendous act of evil that pervaded his world and the lives of millions of others. I'm helpless to solve the world's problems, but I do have the power to do one thing: produce positivity in the form of a letter.

Granddaddy Al (my mother's father) was my first pen pal. He sent letters once a week, always a conglomeration of capitalized verbs and nouns, carefully composed on his portable typewriter. He showed me that there could be joy in sharing the little things and that I didn't have to make big conversation to capture an experience. He slowed down the moment as he embellished things that happened with colorful details.

Nothing was too stupid to write about, he taught me. He related stories as if we were walking around Seattle together, my small hand in his gnarled one as we gathered his cracked crab and sourdough loaves for dinner. Back at 6322 21st Avenue NE, he set the table and waited for the neighbors to join him to break bread, and I was teleported right next to him. Through his letters, I felt warm and included although we were miles apart. (His address jumped into my head sixty years later—it's locked in.)

We corresponded my entire life, so when cancer won and his time was near, my mother and I flew to Seattle to see him in the hospital. I was twenty-five and not a kid anymore, but it was devastating to witness him so pale and weak in his powder blue surgical nightgown. His thin white legs rustled under the sheets when he yanked at the IVs, and monitors clicked and beeped. The scene was a grim reminder of how my strong and hearty grandfather had withered.

As I struggled to stay composed, I saw something familiar: On the flesh-colored swivel table across his bed lay an envelope. It was the one I had mailed the week before, fished out of the well-worn metal mailbox on the porch of his cozy house by a relative and brought here to the ICU. I picked it up off the table and read it to him, choking back tears, knowing full well he would never write back.

When I lost my first pen pal several days after that letter was recited to his weary body, I committed to keeping his spirit alive. I've carried on our tradition with other family and friends and hope I've made Granddaddy Al proud. I mail a thousand bulging envelopes a year, and that number doesn't include packages. Some are for business, and others are personal. My count includes newspaper and magazine clippings, but the net result is that I keep my mailman's hands full. I want everyone to discover the joy of giving and receiving, so my pen pals' ages range from four to ninety-nine. I include candy to incentivize the younger ones to respond—and they turn it around fast! (Don't tell anyone, but it's a great excuse to keep chocolate hidden around the house.)

Thank You note writing did more than help me make my grandfather happy. It also improved my social life from the first interaction with a junior high pen pal—a cute boy with shaggy brown bangs, to be exact. That friend-making technique has expanded my business, too, from the thirty-five-year career I had in television production to what I do now, which is fundraising for universities. Whether you're trying to extend your social circle, reach out to new (or old or cold) contacts, engage new friends, receive special treatment from a restaurant owner, or entice an oblivious crush to notice you, a letter can help you do all of that.

"Thank you" as a concept is far more varied than you might imagine. When they hear "Thank You note," most people think of the stack of responses they are expected to send after the wedding, funeral, bat mitzvah, or child's birthday party. But in this book, I go beyond "thanks for the gift" to "thanks for being you."

For example, when it was evident my mother was near death, it was almost Thanksgiving, and I'd written her a card that included all the things she'd taught me and done for others. Suddenly the moment of her passing was now, and I was flying to her bedside. As I headed out the front door, I realized the carefully crafted homage wouldn't make it to her in time, so I extracted it from my mailbox and brought it with me. When I entered her darkened room, I froze, at a loss about what to do in those sad, final minutes. My sister urged me to read our mom what I'd written, so I recited the two single-spaced typed pages to her. They held all my appreciation for everything she'd taught her four children, for her ethics and politics, and for her belief in the power of the written word. It was the ultimate last Thank You, and it was the last she ever heard. She died twenty minutes later.

I have gone the gamut, from sending written Thank Yous in memoriam to simply enlightening an employee who may not be typically appreciated about how they mattered to me that day. Sometimes I'll send a second note for a gift that keeps on giving, especially for food items or fascinating books. (Christmas cookies from my friends the Trybom-Lucases that I'd stashed in the freezer stayed intact until they were devoured a few months later, and I truthfully told them after opening the white box that I loved their choice even more.) The impact on my recipients is equivalent to the effect on me.

Thank You notes are wonderful if and when there is reciprocity. I've noticed the "art of Thank You" is diminishing year after year, and I worry we're losing a bit of our civility each time we ignore a chance to thank someone for a kindness or say something nice to offset an anonymous cut. We know the haters are

Monday Sept.17th.

Dear Erica:

The "Old Crumb Boss" has finallyy
taken out time to answer one of your many
interesting and lovely letters before you
decide to chastise me by making your "Black
list. It is so easy to get into bad habits
by permitting Nana to take care of the letter
writing and ME do the reading.
Yesterday(Sunday)our good friends
accross the Lake -Marie and Gene Hose had us
to dinner along with mutual friends totaling
twenty in all to a wonderful dinner in celer-
bration of our 59th.wdding Anv .It was a very
wonderful day and the view of the Lake from
their home is just great. Your Mother and Dad
had telegraphed us each a corsage for the day
so you can understand Erice that we went "First
Class" thanks to our wonderful friends and relatives. Also Betty and Gary had telegraphed a
beautiful pot of planted flowers to Mother on
friday and called that evening to converse with
us.I am now pulling hard to make the charmed
"60 year mark" since the 59th. one turned out
so good.

I am so happy for you Erica now that
you own such a wonderful new car and the color
too is my favorite. Not only that but what you
have told us makes us happy that you have also
found a wonderful friend in Jeff and hope some
day to have the good fortune of meeting him too.

I owe Steven a letter and also should
write Kitty but I will confess Erica I get lazy
when the thoughts of writing is concerned. I am
at the present time trying to arrange for someone
to come in for a day each week to help keep this
place presentable as the "Old Crumb Boss" is getting lazier by the week. Nothing more this time
Erica but I want you to know that we love you and
your letters so very very much .
Grandaddy Al

Typed note from
Granddaddy Al.

out there: They're loud, proud, and toxic, trolling the internet to trash whatever or whomever they can for even the smallest perceived slight. Any hateful creep can use their short, grimy fingers to post an ugly, venomous comment. These judgments are hurtful and intended to make people feel bad. I'm moving in the opposite direction, forging a "Civility Campaign" to replace criticism with commendation. In a few keystrokes, you can take the sting out of that hideous feeling and replace it with warm, glowing praise. A bubble bath is infinitely nicer than a cold shower.

I have a few guiding principles about sending out letters that I outline in this book, such as not second-guessing yourself. I figure if I'm the only one going home after a dinner party to thank the hostess, then whatever I send is going to be better than nothing. I preach, "First draft, final draft," and leave it at that. Don't overthink it or you'll freeze and never send it. If you're a parent or grandparent (or aunt or uncle or teacher) and hoping your children or grandchildren, nieces and nephews, or students will be incentivized to pick up a pen or laptop to crank out a letter, I share your frustration about how challenging it is to get this younger generation interested—but I have a few ideas on how to crack the code of indifference. Hint: Candy, cash, and compliments (C-C-C) are part of the equation.

If you're job-seeking and afraid to say the wrong thing after an interview, in all likelihood, you blow it off and do nothing. But I can banish your paralysis.

I've developed a three-paragraph format called "Me, You, and Us" to help get you started, punch up the middle, and finish with a flourish. This formula is easy to follow and works every time.

If you want to ensure someone will put a name to you months after you've sent them a letter, I can embolden you to create such an outreach.

I'm a cheerleader for a vanishing form of etiquette using pre-computer age technology.

If you're intrigued about adding a typewriter back to your workstation, a chapter at the end of this book walks you through what you should consider before you go out and buy one. I've included a few testimonials from friends who caught the fever to help get you excited. Throughout the book, I also weave the "best of" letters I have written and received to exemplify the impact of the Thank You in all its nuances and various forms.

Don't worry—you don't have to learn how to type on a typewriter to enjoy and use this book. All you have to do is be open to the idea of exploring a timeless form of communication in a new way. I predict you'll be thrilled at the results you see in your personal life, professional relationships, and general well-being when you start to write more Thank You notes. The practice is life-expanding and heartwarming.

There's always something or someone to be pleased by if you look around. Challenge yourself—letter writing can be satisfying and mind-expanding. Never mind the joy you'll experience when you think of someone opening up their mailbox and being surprised by your letter. Or, even better, when you look into your pile of bills and circulars and see a letter written to you.

This book is divided into two parts: Part One is about the magic, strength, and happiness behind the Thank You. I'll move into a range of subjects, including how I differentiated myself in my career and personal life by sending Thank You notes.

Those letters landed me jobs and built my brand—and could do the same for you. I'll reveal my philosophy of reciprocity and how genuine kindness communicated on a piece of paper can make you friends and break down barriers.

In Part Two, the real gold is my never-fail approach to a perfect Thank You. You'll get inspired on what to include in a letter via my patented "Three Parts of a Powerful Thank You Note: Me, You, and Us" kick-starter for a fabulous letter every time. (Hint: The magic word is "when.") This approach encourages you to build a beginning, middle, and end to satisfy any reader. It's like crafting a very short story, a love note without the sex talk. The meat of the message is making it "all about you" and shining your light on the person with whom you're communicating.

We'll also review the basics: the equipment you'll need, how to address the envelope, and how to make your product stand out (think USPS stamps and cool stationery—personalized if you get the fever). When you must write something after that important job interview, now you'll know what to say.

What happens beyond the Thank You? How do you spin your skills into money for your company or institution? If you're in fundraising (aka "Advancement" or "Development") for a school, nonprofit organization, or your own business, I share tips on how to persuade the gatekeeper—the assistant—to let you meet their boss for a high-stakes conference. You'll discover how to get in the door to schmooze donors, clients, or patients face-to-face and make your message more electrifying than everyone else's. You will exponentially increase your financial milestones. If you prefer to do this by email, I'll present a structure for that as well.

On the personal scene, there's a section for you, grandparents: If you're desperate to teach your grandkids how to respond to a gift, I've got some ideas for you.

This book will also desensitize you to the "D" word—death. I'll walk you through a delicate approach to adding a personal touch to a purchased condolence card. I know you were hoping the card itself was enough, but if you tailor it to tell a story about the person who died, you will make it even more meaningful.

You'll also learn about me as you become inspired to send your own notes and come to understand why a letter is better. You'll establish stronger relationships in work and in love and become recognized as someone who does things in your own unique way. You'll make an indelible imprint in a society that's flooded with stimuli.

Finally, the book includes a deep dive into how to choose a typewriter for yourself, if you feel so inclined, and testimonials from folks who say that this purchase changed their lives. ●

Why, Thank You

Chapter One

The Magic of Thank You

I love to do something most people hate: write Thank You letters.

To be accurate, I don't handwrite them—I type them. I type Thank You letters to the trash man, the saleslady who finds a sweater for my mom, and the corporate recruiter. I snail mail them to museum directors, college presidents, television producers, celebrities, titans of industry, and plumbers.

My letters stay on desks; people save, frame, or display them. I'll walk into a jewelry repair or a deli and spot my work on the wall. Someone I don't recognize will fly across a crowded room shrieking, "So you're Erica!" and confess they loved my outreach—sent a year ago.

Typed Thank You notes are an icebreaker, a differentiator, my personal brand. Since I'm naturally shy, they're also my bridge to friendship. You don't need to type these notes. You can write, email, or text (my least favorite mode but better than nothing).

If you don't yet practice this old-school form of relating, perhaps when you focus on what this method can provide, you'll be swayed. Written Thank Yous bring power in connection, purpose, and service and add that unique "brand" identification to yourself. People remember if you thank or compliment them. You have an impact on their lives, and they on yours.

My life expanded exponentially after I began letter-writing in earnest. At first, in junior high, I wrote lovestruck letters to would-be boyfriends, hoping for more love in return. It was often a one-way street, but I tried. As I got older, I got bolder, pushing new boundaries, reaching out to strangers, and, as a result, establishing myself on their radar. After a job interview, I've solidified myself as a viable candidate by going home and quickly sending a "thanks for your time" both by email and snail mail—faster and more comprehensively than what my competitors might have produced. I've been promoted, granted access, and made big-money deals because of this practice. After I landed the job, my new boss would elevate me from the herd because they appreciated my Thank You and trusted me to act in a civilized manner of interpersonal connection with vendors, production crews, or donors. Often, once the higher-ups recognized I wasn't afraid, I'd be asked to do more official external communications.

My "second act"—a job in Development/"friend-raising" for a major California university—requires getting in the door to make friends with alums or parents who may be potential donors. My secret weapon? I type my request on a typewriter on a simple piece of paper. The sealed, stamped envelope is then hand-delivered by a representative of the United States Postal Service (USPS). If the "target" I want to meet was trying to ignore me, it's hard to forget a real, live sealed and stamped envelope with a personal plea inside.

One-to-one outreach like this is surprisingly efficient. Although 162.1 million pieces of First-Class Mail are delivered *every day* in the United States (U.S.) (as of March 2023), snail mail still intrigues folks, maybe because of its rarity.

I get a 93 percent open rate—people are blown away when a personalized typed envelope appears in their mailbox.

It's a throwback to another time, an era that has long since disappeared. Lags between each written conversation add suspense to dispatching and then—over the following weeks—waiting for a response. Letter writing makes each interaction much more meaningful and intense. I'll bet very few letters are instantly torn up or burned (as opposed to the impetuous and popular email "Delete").

I get a 93 percent open rate—people are blown away when a personalized typed envelope appears in their mailbox.

The Gilded Age is an American historical drama on HBO Max that showcases how socialites lived, competed for status, and communicated in 1882. I was most intrigued with their formal (and only) method of delivering messages: After Lady of the House #1 handwrote a note and dripped sealing wax on the envelope, her butler placed the note on a silver tray and scurried across the street. House #2's butler accepted the closed envelope and displayed whatever it was—an invitation to tea or a formal fundraiser—on another silver tray for Lady of the House #2. It was formal and charming, and the cursive-written communique was the main event.

A letter is better—it's an immediate personal gift that goes right to the receiver's heart. It's inexpensive, costs less than a dollar, and requires no trekking to stores or searching on Amazon.

Telephones were coming into existence but not yet widely used. I practically swooned when I realized pen and paper were the format of the day, and I pictured myself at a rolltop desk sending out messages to everyone! I would have enjoyed living in that era, where everything was written by hand and transferred (in some cases on silver trays) with care.

Speaking of another time, have you had the pleasure of clearing out an attic or a dusty drawer of your late parents or grandparents? Get ready, because you will be embarking on a journey through history. When you unearth a box of letters a lonely soldier addressed to his beloved wife when he was away on duty, you sense his soul as a man, a husband, and a fighter. You glimpse his fears and relate to the mundane and magnificent or horrific moments he describes. That stack of correspondence is a slow-motion transport into a reality we'll never see.

As you write letters to people, you are adding to their history. Boxes stuffed with scribbled secrets on yellowed paper may be unearthed one day by a family member. That idea may put a slight pause on how detailed you are with your sexy messages! I was deposed once, and the lawyer for the other side threw a stack of white bond paper in my face and asked if I recognized it. I took a look. It was hot-and-heavy suggestive fantasies—all typed, of course—that I'd sent my then-fiancé, Vin Di Bona, over the years. Part of me laughed to myself, though. There, in a courtroom setting, I was asked to claim if I was the author. Of course I was! What a stupid question. Who else would have *typed* erotica? It was utterly mortifying. The letters were then merged into the legal transcript. Wonder what the court stenographer thought of that?

Letters can also find their way back to the originator. I've had many come back to me after the recipient is gone. My friend Darlene Basch introduced me to her mother, Vivian Chakin, when she moved from New York to Los Angeles. Vivian was a Holocaust survivor who generously shared her story with the Shoah Foundation and other groups. She and I developed a warm friendship. We chased down embroidery yarn together so that she could teach me needlework (I was a complete disaster), went to lunch, and cruised the mall looking for bargains. After tea and cookies at her apartment, I would invariably follow up with a note or thanks for the thoughtful gifts she found, many stationery related. After Vivian died, Darlene surprised me with a pyramid of cards her mother had kept—all from me. I was touched that Vivian, who was not a sentimental "saver," had found my love notes important enough to tuck away. Rereading them brought back our happy adventures.

Years later, my ex-husband Josh handed me a sheaf of correspondence I'd sent his late mother, along with rough drafts she'd worked on before she responded. Many people claim they have an "Erica file" because they can't bear to throw my correspondence away. It always embarrasses me to hear that because I am not specifically dropping someone a line with that end goal of "save my epistles" in mind, but I'm satisfied when I hear that I created a happy moment for someone. I hope you'll want to carry that idea forward and be emboldened to craft extra-special messages folks may want to retain after you've read this book!

Where Have All the Letters Gone?

Nowadays, receiving a real, typed envelope with a Thank You inside is unusual, but it used to be the norm. If you're in your sixties, as I am, you most likely took typing class in junior high school. (And no, it wasn't the same as the "keyboarding" computer courses now taught in junior high.) If you're older, you've seen a putty-colored IBM Selectric, a manual Smith-Corona, or a clunky loden green Olympia like the one I learned on, and you remember the effort it took to strike the keys and avoid mistakes. (The "A" on the left-hand side of the keyboard takes extra strength to hit with your pinky finger.)

What else was different back then? Mail delivery was frequent. As a kid, you received holiday, birthday, and graduation cards from your grandparents or godparents with crisp green dollar bills tucked inside. Imagine it's an important day: You skip and sing your way to the gray metal mailbox in front of your home and out tumbles a surprise outreach from a far-away family member who loves you. You race inside, tear open the treasure, and promptly eat, wear, or play with it.

As an adult, the postbox haul isn't as exciting. You get bills and invoices and send back paper checks as payment. I've taught many junior high school kids who have never gotten *anything* in the mail—except one girl, who remembered receiving a postcard for a dental appointment. That's very sad, and it's partly why I've taken on pen pals of all ages. I don't want their mailboxes to gather spiderwebs.

I am not expecting anyone, especially young people, to use longhand to pen a note, and good thing I'm relaxing my expectations since many kids aren't being taught to even *read* cursive. In twenty-one U.S. states, second graders won't learn how to write cursive, and third graders aren't taught how to read words in cursive. (However, California Governor Gavin Newsom signed Assembly Bill 446 on October 13, 2023, so children in first through sixth grade will now be required to learn cursive handwriting in that state.)

As script calligraphy fades from view, using a computer to type a letter is perfectly fine (and I will teach you how to do so in Part Two of this book). In our virtual world, "in real life" contact is even more remarkable and worthwhile, especially as we see it supplanted by texts and tweets. Face it, face-to-face is facing extinction.

Today we're inundated with texts, tweets, Instagram and Facebook DMs, LinkedIn messages, YouTube and TikTok videos, and incessant emails. While any method you choose to get your message across is better than doing nothing at all, texts are usually too brief and lack warmth. They can also be jarring—please don't send big emotional messages, including divorce requests, news of someone's death, or breakups, over text. Handwrite it if your cursive is still legible (mine is not), or compose it on a computer and print it out. Another idea is to use a typewriter, like I do.

It's all the same concept: Memorialize your thoughts on a card or postcard, affix a First-Class stamp, and then send it by snail mail.

If you use a computer, download a font like American Typewriter for a homespun look. (A useful website is *The Classic Typewriter Page: Typewriter Fonts*, created by author Richard Polt.[1] You can also check out font websites such as DaFont.com.) Find a style that speaks to you and adopt it as your "look." Avoid Papyrus or Comic Sans if you have any self-respect! Bad font choices aside, an outreach in *any* format—handwritten, typed, computer generated—sets you apart. People hated the Papyrus font used on the title card of the James Cameron film, *Avatar*, so much that *Saturday Night Live* did a sketch about it.

A letter is better—it's an immediate personal gift that goes right to the receiver's heart. It's inexpensive, costs less than a dollar, and requires no trekking to stores or searching on Amazon.

Think about how you feel when you receive a wrapped package. A stamped envelope is the same, albeit thinner!

Once I walked into the Ralph Lauren Beverly Hills clothing boutique, and upon seeing me, the ladies' belts salesman Vic ordered, "Wait here, I have something to show you," and disappeared to collect his backpack. When he returned, he produced a typed card from me praising his abilities as a salesman. He ran his fingers across his name on the envelope and whispered, "Is it typed?" Then he confessed he had never received something created on a typewriter. I think I saw a tear in his eye. Once again my outreach served us both, as I was delighted to see the pride I had instilled in him from one piece of paper. The next time I wandered into the boutique, Vic noticed

First draft/final draft helps you get over yourself. There's no time for indecision or worrying about every word. Speed is of the essence.

me immediately and gave me a hug, and we were new friends.

Letters may be superior for relationship building (in my estimation), but there are many other outreach options too. I can text, email, or phone—but none of those methods garner as much excitement.

My mantra is: "Letters are better." Composing them has built my identity. They open doors to new relationships in love and at work (what else *is* there) and make you unforgettable to those who work in different venues you frequent, such as stores, restaurants, and doctors' or dentists' offices. Suddenly all the other customers, job applicants, or love interests appear in black and white, and you glow in Technicolor. An acknowledgment boosts endorphins and staves off loneliness—and not just for the person to whom you dropped a note. Surprisingly it's a two-way street. You, too, will feel less lonely after you've made contact. Research has proven that creating and sending a Thank You message makes you happier for *up to two months!*[2] What else has such staying power? It's good for *your* self-esteem and makes *you* memorable.

Letter writing doesn't have to be scary or feel overly important. Don't get stuck. Keep it simple and casual. Plenty of terrific one-liners do the job, as I'll share with you later. Get it done and out the door!

Your rough draft can be your final draft. It's not a school essay; there are no grades. This process doesn't require research or facts and figures. A letter reflects what you're thinking at the moment you disclose it, so it can be as fluid and changeable as your inner world. It can be a mirror into your soul, or you can fake it with "superficial intimacy" and use it as merely a cheery way of connecting. (For those of you not familiar with that term, my former therapist explained it's a way to set boundaries with someone you don't like or trust. The idea is to make them *feel* like you're sharing your innermost thoughts, but you really only

continued:

It is a talent to be able to look at
an ensemble, mull it over for less than
a second & a half, and run back into the
room holding not one but two or even
three solid choices to spark it up. You
take it to the next level, Vic. I hope
to see you soon, and if you're making
any of those delicious butter cookies,
save one for me.

Love,

Erica Di Bona
Erica Di Bona

December 4, 2013

Happy Holidays

Dear Vic --

You are so nice to haVE sent us
this beautiful holiday candle, replete
with a well-tied red bow and maroon,
green & gold decorated box. It's holiday
all over -- and although I haven't yet lit
the candle, I can imagine that given Ralph
Lauren's sensibility, that too will be
a sensuous experience.

I thought of you the other day when I
pulled out that crazy orange belt that we'd
gotten (as an alternative to the green)
for the off-the-shoulder paisley orange/pink/
green/blue silk flowy top and blue pants.
I laughed, thinking about what a good eye
you have -- and how quickly you "see"
what's right.

Holiday card to
Vic at Ralph Lauren.

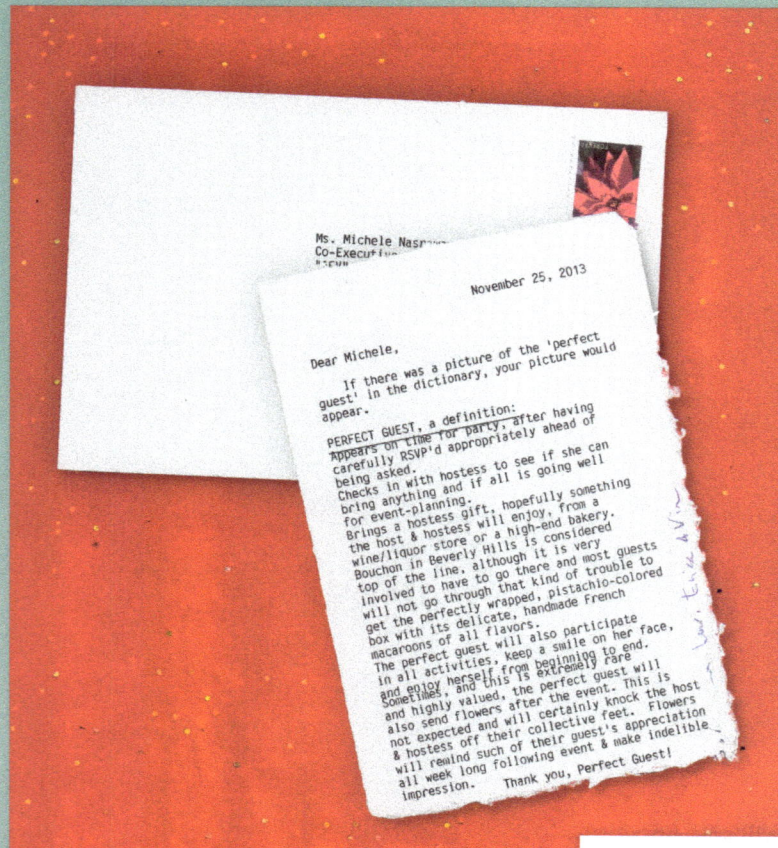

Ms. Michele Nasr...
Co-Executiv...

November 25, 2013

Dear Michele,

If there was a picture of the 'perfect guest' in the dictionary, your picture would appear.

PERFECT GUEST, a definition:
Appears on time for party, after having carefully RSVP'd appropriately ahead of being asked.
Checks in with hostess to see if she can bring anything and if all is going well for event-planning.
Brings a hostess gift, hopefully something the host & hostess will enjoy, from a wine/liquor store or a high-end bakery. Bouchon in Beverly Hills is considered top of the line, although it is very involved to have to go there and most guests will not go through that kind of trouble to get the perfectly wrapped, pistachio-colored box with its delicate, handmade French macaroons of all flavors.
The perfect guest will also participate in all activities, keep a smile on her face, and enjoy herself from beginning to end.
Sometimes, and this is extremely rare and highly valued, the perfect guest will also send flowers after the event. This is not expected and will certainly knock the host & hostess off their collective feet. Flowers will remind such of their guest's appreciation all week long following event & make indelible impression. Thank you, Perfect Guest!

April 29, 2019

Dear Erica,

I just came home to find your beautiful note. It blew me away. The sentiment was very meaningful to me and I thank you truly for taking the time to express those kind thoughts, in the most poetic way.

The party was a gift to all of us who care for Vin to see him lauded, not with another award, but with words of love and admiration from those who know him best. You threw him the best kind of party filled with great food, great friends and non-stop dancing,

but, I think being able to share our feelings about him in a personal setting is what we will remember most.

I did not imagine I would hear such kind words about myself in return and I will strive to continue to earn them. This letter I will keep forever. Thank you, Erica.

Love,
Michele

divulge what is safe for you to say.) Whatever your reason for employing superficial intimacy when you feel guarded, in a protected environment, you will find it's a new "high" to share your feelings and equally enjoyable to send *and* to receive.

When it comes to correspondence, I preach, "One and done." Don't agonize over what you are saying. In college, after sweating over rough draft after rough draft, a lightning bolt struck: The various reports I generated didn't improve much from one to the next, and I was tinkering with tweaks instead of twerking. I was confident enough in my spelling that I didn't flub up there, so I decided to go rogue and trust myself in other areas as well. After I eliminated multiple drafts and committed to the first or second one, I felt liberated. I wouldn't recommend this gunslinger "method" to everyone, though. It's good if you've been writing recently and you're all warmed up. Otherwise, create a few drafts if you must, but pay attention to how much you repair your work.

A common expression says, "You have to throw out the first pancake." It's the experimental batter drop to see if the concoction is the right texture, if the heat's where it needs to be, and if it's ready for mass production. Like a first pancake, if your letter is less than perfect but not burned to a crisp, you can decide whether to toss it in the garbage or send it "as is." I guarantee you are far more critical of your work than the recipient, who's excited to get something—anything—in the mail. You may bemoan the first pancake as an unappetizing mess, but nobody else will judge you as harshly as you condemn yourself.

First draft/final draft helps you get over yourself. There's no time for indecision or worrying about every word. Speed is of the essence.

After I've been in someone's home, I want to reach my hosts while the memory is fresh. Once my husband Vin and I threw a cocktail party for a Catholic television production group, and two days later, my mailbox was full—every guest had dashed off a lovely note. I figured they must have all driven home and headed right to their desks because there was zero lag time. (We had a full-service bar with full-strength cocktails, so after two hours of booze before the meal, our guests were feeling no pain!) It was an astonishing feat to receive a hundred percent return on investment. That's a cohort I'd invite again! Talk about exquisite manners. They were the most grateful visitors ever.

You can also think outside of the box, or as my friend Rhode Island School of Design Trustee Emeritus Richard Haining always says, "Think as if there *is* no box." It doesn't always have to be "guests write to host." It can be the other way around, too, where you—the event host—let the guests know how much you enjoyed having them at your party. Wouldn't it be cool to get a "best guest ever" note?

Vin's Co-Executive Producer from *America's Funniest Videos*, Michele Nasraway, was one such guest at a dinner party we threw. In a note, I created a "Perfect Guest" definition that outlined all those responsibilities—and said she'd met every single one.

She then wrote me a beautiful Thank You card back saying she was touched, which touched

I want you to feel seen and appreciated, even if nobody else reminds you how special you are.

me in turn. This is the reciprocity of Thank You in action.

Good results start from one action, one envelope, and one USPS Forever® stamp. We need to see and appreciate each other, and while it's pleasant to collect compliments by text or in person, nothing is as soul-touching as securing a letter in the mail.

I'm no Paul Smith, the "Typewriter Artist" with cerebral palsy who was born in 1921. He didn't speak until age sixteen, after his parents gifted him a typewriter hoping it might help him write (since he never received a proper education). Much to everyone's surprise, he found another form of expression. He began to "paint with a manual typewriter"—he created art by rolling the paper up and down the typewriter's carriage, then going across the page and striking it with letters and symbols. (Paul is a hero in the typewriter world.)

I can't execute such elaborate designs, but when I sit at my putty-colored Olympia Electronic Compact 2, circa 1983, my goal is also to bestow a treasure you'll keep when times are rough. I want you to feel *seen* and *appreciated*, even if nobody else reminds you how special you are—*especially* if nobody else reminds you.

Oprah Winfrey, one of the best television interviewers of our era, discovered that simple truth after talking to nearly 30,000 people on her show. She concluded that "all 30,000 had one thing in common. They all wanted validation." It's the simple act of "letting people know, 'I see you. I hear you. And what you say matters.'"[3]

Oprah's show delivered that message to her guests and in turn to her audience. It was "the validation of the voiceless." The voiceless concept hits home for me. I grew up feeling crowded out by my younger sisters and as if I didn't have a voice. When I was three, I stopped talking altogether for a time after my two younger sisters were born within thirteen months of each other. I didn't consciously know it but sensed there was no place for me. So I'm giving you what I wish I bathed in back then—undivided attention, love, and simple appreciation for who you are and what you mean to me. This is my cathartic fix for my lonely, nonverbal years!

Here is the truth about letter writing and thanking others: It pays double dividends. But how?

Courage—It gives you a voice to ask for what you want and not be overly attached to results. You can use this format to crack the code on a cool new friend you want to get to know better or to convince a businessperson you're "not the average bear," as my oral surgeon once told me. (I needed more painkillers than most!)

Reciprocity—A Thank You is as much a gift for the recipient as it is for me. It can be a two-way exchange, even if you didn't start with that goal. There is altruism in the desire to be of service. It's not about me, it's about *you*. But here's the irony: I find so much gratification in making people happy with my love letters that after sending one, more love flows back into *my* heart. It's a boomerang effect. I claim to be altruistic and create my love bombs with no expectations, but the dirty

> My words immediately set me apart and keep my name on the tip of their tongue a day longer.

little secret is that, in my heart of hearts, I wish someone would do the same for me. When I'm having a rough day, if I open my mailbox and several unexpected envelopes tumble out, my spirits instantly lift. I *do* matter. Someone was thinking of me, wanted to connect, and took the time to share their feelings.

Purpose—You can be a harbinger of peace. Take a measurable action step toward your desire for "People, can't we all just get along?" (to quote Rodney King after the Los Angeles riots in 1992). As a society, I dream of a day when "the pen is mightier than the sword"—when we demonstrate our desire for peace and civility, when we prioritize kindness over killing. As people in various countries worldwide, including the U.S., are busy blowing each other up, isn't it time to exchange love instead of foment hate?

During the COVID-19 pandemic, pen pal clubs sprang up across the continent, and major organizations like United Way got in the mix to match lonely seniors with eager correspondents to help their mental and physical well-being. Love through the mail was a reminder other people cared. Penpalooza launched online on Elfster—originally designed to help with Secret Santa gift exchanges—and the idea exploded. By the end of 2020, nine thousand pen pals had been matched with connections from fifty-plus countries. Elfster had to re-engineer their code due to the high demand! Additionally, International Pen Friends,[4] founded in 1967, claims to have nearly three million members, comprising kids, youth groups, and adults. Clearly, the organization has tapped into a deep-seated need.

Connection—It's a tangible reminder of how vital it is to feel connected. Scientific studies have proven that lonely people die sooner than those who *belong to* a community. Being a pen pal with someone, whether older or younger, isn't the same as being together in person, but

Dear Erica,
I loved getting your typed letter! Thanks for getting in touch! I would type you back but my beauty is sitting in my dad's basement waiting to get fixed "one of these days." I'm signed up to teach at RISD next Spring in the Illustration dept. and couldn't be more excited. I am enclosing some typewriter temporary tattoos to add to your collection :) I also have a whole line of typewriter related fabric with Windham Fabrics if you ever think of sewing something. Keep in touch!
Warmly, Julia Rothman

Handwritten card from Julia Rothman.

it reminds them that you are thinking of them. According to the 2022 Cigna Group report on the "loneliness epidemic," 57 percent of men and 59 percent of women reported being lonely. Most young men in their twenties are single, according to psychologist Greg Matos, who suggests they consider getting therapy, valuing their internal world, and respecting their ideas to communicate them effectively.[5]

What better approach to chip away at feeling isolated and alone than to bare your soul on paper? What's less risky than that? If you're not sure of your subject matter, generate a few versions until you're happy with it. When you hide behind the written word, you can take your time as you spell it out. You won't freeze, mumble, or forget what you want to say. You gain control of the communication. In the dating world, being "large and in charge" can liberate you.

Even texts are challenging to structure for the best results. There are tutors on how to compose the most attention-grabbing come-ons via text. (Dating by Blaine with Blaine Anderson, who specializes in helping men, attracted mogul Mark Cuban as her investor on ABC's *Shark Tank*.)[6] It all comes down to how you market yourself to sell the "message of you."

Ditch the dating apps—here's a low-tech workaround from centuries ago. Have you read about the seventeenth-century silver-tongued soldier Cyrano de Bergerac? Despite his huge nose and unfortunate looks, he wooed the beautiful Roxane, not for himself (although he ended up falling in love with her) but for another fellow named Christian. The written word can attract any lover, even from afar. Witty and beautiful—and seemingly unapproachable—cousin Roxane is a famous example. (Spoiler alert: It's a tragedy because Cyrano doesn't get the girl; Christian does. But Roxane asks Cyrano to protect Christian and make sure he writes her every day, so we learn she unknowingly fell in love with the prose of the guy with the big nose. Psych!)

Service—It keeps me part of something bigger than myself. When I do my job as a "friend-raiser," I'm keenly aware that I represent a university or nonprofit organization, and I hope to show my affiliation in the best possible light. I'm the first impression the alum or donor has of the place I'm fronting, and it may have been decades since they were last approached by anyone—if at all.

My outreach must be memorable. I'm convinced that this is where my typed messages beat out every other form of communication. First, I write a letter to introduce myself and the university or organization to the person I hope to meet. Once we connect, I'm like Customer Service, there to handle the grudges or complaints an alum may feel for not having been included or valued up to this point. If that's the case, I tailor my letters to let them vent, try to redress their concerns or solve sticky situations, and help them move forward with goodwill and renewed interest.

Identification—This is my brand. When I tell someone I type letters, most folks are curious, and some work up the courage to ask, "Would you write one to me?" I always say yes. Sometimes they'll start to recite their email address, and I correct them mid-sentence. "Snail mail!" I bark, and it takes a second for it to sink in. It's a token of our budding friendship. I've followed up with many people after meeting them once to say, "It was great talking last night and I look forward to our next conversation." My words immediately set me apart and keep my name on the tip of their tongue a day longer, and every time I send a real-life follow-up note, I'm fairly certain I'm the only one doing that! It makes a cocktail party more fun, too, if during the course of our conversation it comes up that I still type letters. I always promise to send one, and it jet-propels our chance meeting into a deeper rapport.

Julia Rothman is a well-known illustrator who features drawings of office supplies on notebooks and journals. I bought a lined journal because it made me happy to see pens, paper, and staplers getting their due, and I wanted to let her know. I tracked down Julia's studio in New York and wrote a fan letter. She replied and included a few typewriter temporary tattoos, and years later, I was at a Rhode Island School of Design gathering in Manhattan when my hostess sidled up to me to say Julia Rothman was across the room and would I like to meet her? The illustrator remembered our exchange, and the ice was broken in a lovely way.

I understand that for some of you, this idea of creating snail mail will be new and might add another time-consuming task to your already hectic life. Yet once you connect the dots and experience increased connectivity after writing a few letters and spreading some Thank You cheer, you will see letter writing is something you want to integrate as a weekly practice for its mental health benefits.

If you feel resistance to sharing more Thank Yous, let down your defenses, lean in, and begin. If any letters or ideas within this book get you jazzed, please "borrow" them. I know this is not the only book about Thank Yous that's on the market, and several have hard and fast rules about the "right way" to do it. Some of those books scare me, to tell you the truth.

Get ready for a shocker: I proclaim you don't have to follow the old standard of handwriting a letter. Many of us don't use cursive at all, and some of us never learned to write or read it. Your grandmother would have been horrified at my advice; she would consider it poor etiquette. She likely urged you to express gratitude, and on that, Granny was right. Where Granny and I disagree is on *form,* not *function.* I'm saying you don't need to know cursive and have perfect penmanship. Make it easy on yourself. Do what comes naturally—if the production plan is too daunting, you'll give up before you even begin. You can use your computer to compose your letter and print it out. Be less formal and have more fun. If you're only emotionally capable of taking a picture on your phone and texting it to the person who sent you those flowers, then do that. Show yourself holding the bouquet or sniffing the flowers as you put the blooms into a vase.

There's also the one-sentence Thank You note that is *very* short and sweet. Think inside the box—include a happy message about how you appreciate the person for what they did for you or what gift they gave—but think outside the

> **If you feel resistance to sharing more Thank Yous, let down your defenses and begin let down your defenses, lean in, and begin.**

box too. How could you slam this together in one sentence and communicate your message? Be creative, casual, and conversational.

Bring the giver into the moment with you, just as my Granddaddy Al virtually incorporated me into his dinner party by sharing all the details of how he bought the best Dungeness crab and softest sourdough for his seafood feast. He didn't have a smartphone, and this was decades before Polaroids had been invented, but he created vivid visual snapshots as he munched his dinner. And through his descriptions, I was right there with him.

I'm probably the only "Thank You expert" who encourages you to be yourself. Write it once for effect, use my easy prompts, and see how generative adding this soft skill can be for you and your friend, family, and work relationships. I *want* you to use and abuse these concepts. What's mine is yours.

As Michael J. Fox said, "If you don't think you have anything to be grateful for, keep looking. Because you don't just receive optimism. You can't wait for things to be great and then be grateful for that. You've got to behave in a way that promotes that."

So—start behaving.

Chapter Two

The Strength of Thank You

People are out there trying to reinvent the wheel on how to get ahead, but meanwhile the humble Thank You strategy is an overlooked gem because of its seemingly archaic origin. After introducing one of the first "self-help" books in the late 1930s, Dale Carnegie taught courses on how to win friends and influence people (also the name of his book)[7] and discussed "10 Ways to Make People Like You." Four of them are components of the Thank You or acknowledgment of others:

- **Be generous with praise**
- **Remember their name**
- **Be genuinely interested in other people**
- **Know the value of charm**

Sinclair Lewis, a novelist and the first American author to win the Nobel Prize in Literature, was known for his acerbic wit. He weighed in with his own opinion of the technique a year after Carnegie's book was published. He charged it taught people to "smile and bob and pretend to be interested in other people's hobbies precisely so that you may screw things out of them."

If what you do is disingenuous, Sinclair Lewis is right—it *is* a see-through "suck-up." Where so many modern-day formats of correspondence are simply ways to get tasks "off the list" with little thought behind them, we are more in peril of a lack of disconnection than being fake. A written Thank You, however, leaves a remnant of thought and consideration. It's an opportunity to have a voice, confidence, and courage in an indelible way that doesn't require showing up in person or becoming more persuasive. A letter can be your avatar: You are present in the reader's mind without your actually being there. A letter guarantees more staying power than a Zoom call or a FaceTime.

When you reread a letter, it summons a flood of endorphins almost as pleasant as those from a repeat experience. Some folks like to keep their cards and letters so that on a down day, a glance at those keepsakes will lift them out of their sad mood. A letter can evoke the senses and bring the gift-giver into the room with you. It can describe the smell of the gardenias you welcomed for your birthday, the touch of the masseuse you booked with the spa gift card you were given, or the page-turning suspense of a new mystery novel your pal found. When we write a letter, it holds the power of seeing an experience from another perspective. The paper communique is frozen in time. It's a snapshot of what was going on at the time, and when you reread it later, it reminds you of all those emotions.

A letter is a time machine with the power to transport you from the present to the past, giving you a chance to relish and relive that experience.

With the desire to differentiate yourself and an open mind, if you try good old-fashioned letter writing, here are some of the perks you may experience:

- You'll gain the confidence to send your thoughts to a celebrity, a potential employer, or a special person with whom you want to connect.
- You'll differentiate yourself with written outreach as your "brand."
- You'll discover how far a letter propels you in the business world.
- You'll kick down doors and make powerful connections.
- You'll have a method to teach your children—or grandchildren—how to scratch out a message of gratitude.
- You'll catapult your résumé to the top of red-starred emails.

> When you reread a letter, it summons a flood of endorphins almost as pleasant as those from a repeat experience. Some folks like to keep their cards and letters so that on a down day, a glance at those keepsakes will lift them out of their sad mood.

I finally have the guts to tackle it and your recipe will be used.
Thanks again

Lynda Levy

Dear Mr. Gerard,
Thanks for allowing Erica to send me your cookbook. I really appreciate it. We have gotten addicted to the cooking channel and now I look forward to making some of your recipes. I've owned a fish poacher for 30 years and was afraid to use it.

Letter to Lynda Levy from Dad.

- You'll make a huge impact and create a treasure that will linger on someone's desk or bedside table, be framed on the wall, or be tucked in a file.
- You'll achieve the joy of reaching out to another person.
- You'll experience psychological and physical euphoria from doing a good deed.
- Your health will improve, and you'll sleep better, experience less stress, and lower your risk for depression, generalized anxiety disorder, phobias, nicotine dependence, alcohol dependence, and drug abuse.

For example, I once wrote John Landgraf, the chairman of FX Networks, and nine months later, a manila envelope with "FX" in the upper left corner appeared. He admitted my note had been on his desk all this time and apologized for not getting back to me sooner. I was excited he wrote at all—that is the mark of a caring executive. When I met his wife, actress Ally Walker, I mentioned how impressed and surprised I'd been at his actions. She revealed he was scrupulous about responding to a letter and would always do so when called upon.

Moral of the story: Emails get buried under seas of other emails, but a letter on a desk is eternal!

My father, Gary Gerard, taught me that the more charm you could lay on someone, the better. He was also a very generous man. He created a cookbook called *Cooking for Vin* and loved gifting it to solidify relationships. He sent one to my friend Lynda Levy, and her response meant enough that he wrote her back—and then sent me the exchange. I liked his cordial beginning: "Dear Lynda Levy."

Harold is a powerful speaker, and when I joined Toastmasters, club members told me he had won every championship in sight and proudly sported a thirty-year badge. To look at Harold, you wouldn't expect it; he was pear-shaped, wore glasses that skidded down his nose, and was always shoving his button-down shirt into his pants. He was the featured speaker one evening and related a brutally honest story about the darkest night of his soul: He saw a pair of lovers on a bench near where he planned to roll his car down a cliff and, in a last-minute decision, decided he didn't want to traumatize them.

He backed away from the edge and returned to his dorm. He lost weight, studied hard, and moved forward in life. After his narrative, I got his business card so that I could write him. A week later—saying nobody in all his years

Expressing your true and often unexpressed feelings is a skill that builds confidence in your voice and purpose. It gives you an opportunity to be your best self. Maybe you were afraid to give that compliment face-to-face or you didn't say it when you could have, so now that opportunity is in the rearview mirror.

had ever done that before—he displayed the envelope from my letter to the group. Fast forward some months later, and he showed the group the letter again. He carried it around in his blue backpack as a talisman of good luck, a reminder that someone cared.

Building Impactful, Lasting Relationships

Making an impact and cementing the relationship is a huge plus in the financial industry as well as in real estate.

Money management companies demand an extra-personal touch from their employees. Wall Street stockbrokers and business managers are required to communicate with the clients who entrust them with their money. A former partner at the Goldman Sachs investment banking company in New York, showed me a company he'd invested in—it used a person's handwriting sample to generate client letters that looked and sounded genuine. He was pleased because it saved him hours of toil. He was willing to outsource the client outreach correspondence because nobody would guess it wasn't directly from him. His handwriting was imitated down to the last crossed "t." It was both fascinating and fear-inducing to think one's individuality could be copied that easily.

As I write this, I've received a surprise package from my late mother's stockbroker, who handwrote a gracious message and included a thermos coffee cup and elderberry-flavored Sugarfina gummy bears, all branded with her corporate logo. With her kind gesture, she's succeeded in reassuring me it was a good choice to trust her—plus I'm advertising her for free as I walk around holding her thermos.

Letters of appreciation are not limited to the financial world. Realtors can further catapult their relationships by sending Thank You notes after the initial agreement and the sale and to the mortgage broker. Anyone whose business includes signing a contract with mutual trust can add this tactic to their arsenal.

There is always room for Thank You!

Expressing Your Truth

Expressing your true and often *unexpressed* feelings is a skill that builds confidence in your voice and purpose. It gives you an opportunity to be your best self. Maybe you were afraid to give that compliment face-to-face or you didn't say it when you could have, so now that opportunity is in the rearview mirror. You can clamber back into that person's good graces, though. A letter places you in front of them again, virtually, and is a powerful yet nonthreatening way to express yourself. If you transmit a letter, you are committing to a lasting format, which makes your move even more courageous.

One of the Scariest Letters I Ever Wrote—Norman Lear

Norman Lear was a legendary television producer, a quadruple-hyphenate actor-writer-producer-director who still made shows at age 101. He created *All in the Family, Good Times, Sanford and Son, The Jeffersons, Maude,* and *American Masters* and since 2017 had been undertaking *live* remakes of *One Day at a Time, Who's the Boss?* and the Netflix special *Good Times*.

When Emerson College, based in Boston, built a Hollywood outpost for its film and television students, Norman happily reconnected with his alma mater. In 2004, he and his wife invited us to a party at their home above Bel Air. I took a flute of champagne, wandered over to gaze at the canyon and tiny dollhouses below, and realized: *At one point, almost everyone in the country—maybe even the people in those houses—had watched Norman Lear's shows.* At dinner, we talked about academia. Larry David, a comedian, writer, producer, and Emerson parent, sat at the president's table. We felt exalted by the company.

At home that night, I began to compose Mr. Lear a message but froze before I'd even begun. "Don't be afraid," I lectured myself. "Who else is *typewriting* him a letter right now?" Of that I could be sure—only me. What unmitigated gall! How dare I say *anything* to this genius who oversaw the best and brightest television scriptwriters. I forged ahead, clutched my figurative pearls, and placed the letter in the outgoing mail.

A few days later there was a message on my home answering machine. (Some of you may not know about those: They were mini cassettes in a machine that constantly broke down but were supposed to record incoming calls for posterity.)

"Erica, it is Norman Lear. I ... this is such a beautiful letter I received from you, and I've tried to answer it ... but I'm taking the easy way out by calling you ... and because the letter's so beautiful and I don't want to try to write another one—I wish you'd call me" ...[He gives me his phone number.] *"Thanks, dear."*

I shrieked and played it for Vin, then transcribed it word for word. The next morning, though not too early, I called the man himself and babbled about how much he meant to television—and to me.

We have lost the thread of action and individuation and are ensnared by instant gratification. Everything, even finding love, is quicker. Tinder arrived on the app scene in 2012, and it's since taught us well: You can scroll through dozens of suggested love and sex matches faster than it takes to fill your car with a tank of gas (or charge it with electricity). Swipe right if you like, swipe left to reject. No more hand-scratched workout routines on a notepad—wear an Apple watch that tracks your every move. Why take tedious trips to the stores when you can shop online? Want a navy blue sweatshirt? Order it on online and never leave your comfortable couch.

Erica Gerard Di Bona

May 23, 2014

Dear Norman and Lyn,

The first thing we both talked about when we woke up this morning was -- "Wasn't that a perfect party at Norman   house last night?"

You had everything coordinated -- from the dramatic drop & unveil of the screen (which Vin called the "Goldfinger" moment) -- to the speech you made after dinner ... we all felt enveloped in the warmth of your mutual embrace.

But it went deeper than that. Yes, the drinks on the terrace were a spectacular overview of our fair city. Yes, the dinner itself was delicious -- I could have eaten the leafy salad as an entire meal! -- but it went further than the food & libations.

You invoked the grandeur of Hollywood and reminded us all of the dream we come here to achieve. You inspired the young, newly-minted graduates who have their careers ahead of them. You reminded us why we slog away, why we need to craft television that makes a difference. You took us to a higher level -- while reminding us that you, too, Norman, were once a fellow who worried if he'd fit in... and your creativity, work ethic, dynamism and productivity sailed you to the top of the mountain, both literally and figuratively.

Thank you for sharing your living room with us. For opening your home & your hearts -- and for honoring Emerson College and all its constituents in such a meaningful night.
Best,

Erica & Vin Di Bona
Erica & Vin Di Bona

Check out my blog: ArtofThankYou.com

Letter to
Norman Lear.

There are *many* stories of successful people who have written letters about their dreams and how they have hit home. And you will get rejections or no one will respond, but you are still taking action to manifest something else to come.

The Thank You note is an undercover missile launch. It's the best-kept secret. Don't disappear into the crowd of emails when you can stand out with snail mail. It is worth the wait for the letter to land, and you may be surprised by the results.

Receiving Hope

I have been on the receiving end of the Thank You at a time in my life when I needed affirmation as a young woman starting off in the entertainment industry.

You Matter—Note from Connie Chung

Connie Chung, a glamorous anchorwoman, once praised me for my hard work. I was straight out of college and green, green, green. I was in awe of Connie. It was the early 1970s, and she had come from Washington, D.C., where she was the correspondent for *CBS Evening News with Walter Cronkite*. She was the second woman and first Asian person to anchor a major nightly news program. (She went on to work for ABC, NBC, CNN, and MSNBC in addition to CBS.) She was a national role model of what an Asian woman could achieve; immigrant families from China who wanted their daughters to also succeed would name their girls "Connie."

So when she noticed me—the lowly bagel girl who hoped to go out in the field one day for more than New York–style bialys—I was beyond

Hi Erica—
July 28, 1980
You know how much I love you —and I just want to thank you for spending a great Saturday night with our gang. I am so glad and so happy about that night. What fun! We will always work together.
Love, Connie

○ Card from Connie Chung.

thrilled. She praised me for working hard, and along with the crew, we went all around various cities when she co-hosted the first year of the TV show *2 on the Town*. She let me know that she had done what I was doing and that there would be an upside if I stuck with it. It might have seemed like an endless slog, but little by little, I was strengthening my research and logistical skills.

Connie also sent me this note, which meant everything to me. Suddenly I wasn't struggling to master the big world—I *mattered*. I tucked the envelope away so that I could pull it out if and when I doubted myself. It became my reminder that I could keep going, and it carried me through some tough situations. I vowed that one day I would pay it forward and encourage another young production assistant for *their* hard work.

What Connie did in her short note was give me the confidence that allowed me to take on a career in entertainment that spanned thirty-five years.

Connection Through the Holidays

My hands literally ache by the end of the holidays because I've sent Christmas and Hanukkah cards to all the folks I want to thank for interacting with me during the year. I type a personalized message, usually on a pop-up card. People save and look forward to them. (One fellow board member let me know she's moving and wanted me to have her current address so that she wouldn't miss any missives.)

I often write something basic like, "Thanks for being a nice person." During the holidays I send gregarious greetings to folks I don't talk to all the time. One of those exchanges occurred after my sister Annie and I rediscovered Mr. Silvers, our beloved fourth-grade teacher who still

> The Thank You note is an undercover missile launch. It's the best-kept secret. Don't disappear into the crowd of emails when you can stand out with snail mail.

resided in our hometown of Palo Alto, California. I sent him a typed holiday card thanking him for the impact he had on my life in elementary school. He responded with a hand-illustrated card, and we warmed up our relationship as adults, decades after our teacher–student days.

Deserving of Multiple Thank Yous

Sometimes one person deserves to be thanked more than once.

Dr. Irving Posalski is a well-known doctor who has treated two men in my life—but I've never met him. I have, however, written him twice.

My father almost died from two different types of virulent infections after both of his knee replacements. At ninety-six years old, he was too ill to travel, so my internist suggested a second

Correspondence with Mr. Silvers.

Dear Mr. Silvers:
There are some things in life we just don't forget. Your handwriting, for one. Its bold blue line, like Harold & the purple crayon, that when I see it, I know it promises a link to my happy fourth grade year with you, when I was "Eggy" and you found my heart.
When I see your handwriting, I am right back there in that hard wooden seat again. I'm in the comfort of your classroom, excited by what you're showing us, hanging on your every word. I am with what I will know later will be one of my most formative teachers of my career. I'm with someone --you -- who "sees" me,

WARMEST WISHES FOR A
HAPPY HOLIDAY SEASON

past the big, uncomfortable nose that mars my confidence; past the older sibling who doesn't get to play; past the myriad of insecurities, you find me underneath all that, and bring me out of my shell. And for that kindness & insight, Mr. Silvers, you will also be MY GIFT -- and you undoubtedly are told this all the time but let me add my love & thanks and gratitude to the pile: you saved me.
Love, Love, Erica Gerard DiBona

Erica "Eggy" Gerard (now Di Bona)
12-17-14

opinion from the best infectious disease doctor he knew in Southern California.

On the phone, I explained that my father was a Holocaust survivor and a fighter but that this siege might take him out. The doctor promised to review the paperwork about the surgeries and check my dad's medications. I hired a medical social worker to track the paperwork down, and she found over six hundred files from one year's worth of appointments. We sent the disc to the doctor.

The night before Yom Kippur, the holiest day in the Jewish calendar, Dr. Posalski called. I jotted down notes as quickly as I could. We were doing some things right, but he suggested changes in drugs. When I offered to pay, he waved me away. It was the holidays, he said, and he was honored to do a mitzvah (good deed) for a survivor. I hung up and cried. Daddy's illness had been a long journey, fraught with disaster, and here, in a single transaction, was kindness and clarity.

With new meds, my father rapidly recovered. I never imagined that four years later, I'd request another miracle from the same doctor.

Recently, my husband developed internal problems. We were at his urologist's office when his doctor suggested an infectious disease team. Vin had already seen one group to no avail.

"How about Dr. Posalski?" I pitched again, having been ignored before. This time, sensing my frustration, Vin's urologist agreed.

I didn't join Vin because I had a work conflict. I was bummed, but the night before, I had a flash of inspiration. My father had lived several extra years thanks to this humanitarian. I ran to my typewriter and rattled out a letter.

"Give it to him before you start the exam." I thrust the envelope into Vin's hands. Once in the sterile exam room, Vin did just that. The physician read my letter. He remembered the case, he said, and appreciated hearing the update. Dr. Posalski solved Vin's mysterious ailment too.

A doctor may seem like God, but truly, they are a mere mortal. When you let them know they guided you back to good health, they will appreciate it.

Postscript: Dr. Posalski showed the praise to his wife, who proclaimed, "We *know* those people!" We'd attended a party at the home of mutual friends years before, but it took my message to figure that out.

Each note you write makes the next one easier. You've surely heard of "muscle memory" when you're training in the gym. With Thank You writing, you are incrementally building your reflexive writing muscle each time until you begin to do it more regularly. Jimmy Fallon hand-scrawls his weekly "Thank You Notes" segment on *The Tonight Show* (NBC) on Thursday nights, which takes ten seconds. Although it's a joke, the message is that nothing is too small to acknowledge. He'll write, "Thank you, cotton candy, for making my grandmother's hair look delicious," or, "Thank you, bowling, for giving me an excuse to drink with someone else's shoes on."

"Feeling unappreciated is the #1 reason people leave their jobs and their relationships," Mark Zuckerberg, founder and CEO of Facebook (now Meta), once said when he'd decided his top New Year's resolution was to write a Thank You note every day. If a CEO can find a hidden pocket of time every week, so can you. Grab ten minutes while you're on hold for a Zoom meeting or call to begin. If you ride the train, take a few pre-stamped notecards on your commute. Write a note once a week, say on a Friday, to wrap things up with a positive outreach.

In an article, Guy Trebay of *The New York Times* once wrote that "hand-written thank you notes are 'experiencing a moment of vogue' and writing them is 'on trend.'"[8]

The strengths of written correspondence are vast: You have the emotional real estate to share how you feel without fear of interruption or repercussion. It's a work-around for those of us who don't relish direct confrontation. You can stand up for yourself without being nose to nose. If you've made a mistake and want to apologize, you can say, "I'm sorry," from a distance. (True confession: I've done that many times when I was too chickenshit to do it in person.)

A letter can also defuse a tense situation. While you pull back to take a literal breath, you have time to rewind the scenario in your head. We don't always know how we feel in any given moment, but writing a letter instead of shooting off a hasty email or twisted text message gives you extra time before you go DEFCON 4. It pauses the fury, slows down the rapid-fire exchange of emotions, and gives you time to reflect.

So, what's the bottom line with Thank Yous? Whether you believe it or not, they are pertinent: To get anywhere, you need to dream up a way to stand out from the crowd in our noisy world. ●

Chapter Three

You Can Never Go Wrong with Thank You

Writing a Thank You note and then finding out the recipient loved or appreciated it works both ways. I feel good when someone acknowledges that my words meant something to them. Am I suggesting you write a Thank You to receive a Thank You? Well, why not?

If you don't write someone back, you stop the flow of happiness and cut off the potential for a long-lasting correspondence. There are worse events in the world than a seemingly never-ending chain of letters—but that's just me talking.

Have you ever labored over a sensitively composed love note or message by mail or email and received crickets in return? It's a gut punch, isn't it? While the intent is not for us to *be* the recipient, admit it: We do write these cards and letters to also satisfy our own egos. We hope it will become a treasure that spills out of their mailbox, a talisman of a budding friendship, romance, or working relationship.

We all want to be acknowledged if we put our heart on our sleeve and make ourselves vulnerable in written form as we try to deepen relationships with our friends, romantic partners, boss, co-workers or team, as well as build greater trust with those around us. We're hardwired for "give and take."

Five components of a healthy relationship include conversation, mutual help, awarding compliments, accepting someone's flaws, and giving space; letters can cover the first three.[9]

According to Caren Merrick, "Writing thank you letters is one of the easiest ways to give and receive huge benefits, from boosting someone's self-esteem (and knowing you put a smile on their face) to building relationships and trust that have a beneficial ripple effect for years to come."[10]

Bliss hides in Thank You exchanges. "What goes around, comes around." You get a hit of happiness by thanking another person, and being kind to yourself each day has a healing effect too. A natural mood enhancer, you have the power to impart that important free gift to someone. If you appreciate it when the other person does you a favor, does it improve your mood? Do you tell them? I'll bet you consider it for a hot second, then blow it off and go on to dinner.

So the burning question is, why didn't you take a moment to let them know? If you

To be grateful boosts our happiness and health. Look around and you'll see gratitude journals and apps everywhere.

knew that comment could improve interpersonal relationships both at home *and* at work, would that be enticing enough? If you thought it could have the same effect on your nervous system as a glass of wine, a vape hit, or a cigarette drag when you're feeling tense, would you try a note instead of a toke to feel pleasure and contentment?

Fortunately, after I've written someone, I usually get a response. Days, weeks, or months later, I'll walk into a party, restaurant, or store, and someone I don't recognize will rush over to burble about how my message meant so much to them, then ask shyly, "Was it typed?"

When a "rusher" appears, my husband takes it for granted because it's so common. He shakes his head and murmurs, "She writes great letters, doesn't she?" Vin doesn't realize this is a sacred moment.

In our exchange, my recipient and I share our truths and deepen our relationship. As in any intimate ritual, we are consecrated unto each other.

Just as I make *you* feel special, I want you to appreciate *me*. That tongue-tied teenage girl is still living inside me, hoping someone will notice her.

The Thank You Letter Is a Form of Gratitude

"Gratitude" is a big buzzword. To be grateful boosts our happiness and health. Look around and you'll see gratitude journals and apps everywhere. Laurie Santos, a psychologist who teaches about well-being and happiness at Yale University, says, "Those type of products can remind us to take time to be grateful. But it's also important to remember that *gratitude is free.*" And not only is it free but it can also have long-term positive effects on your mental health.

> ## "Gratitude can transform common days into thanksgiving, turn routine jobs into joy, and change ordinary opportunities into blessings."
> —Old Proverb

Dr. Santos asked her students "to write a thank you letter and then read it out loud to the recipient. I can show measurable improvements in well-being even a month after (they've) done this," she reported. One letter read out loud lasts for a month? What tonic can promise *that*?[11]

The principle that lies behind this concept is gratitude, which comes from the Latin word "gratia," meaning—surprise, surprise—gratefulness or thankfulness. So gratitude refers to a "state of thankfulness" or "of being grateful." Hardly anyone gets thanked for the little stuff, so they are always surprised when they are. You benefit greatly from their glee.

A proverb says, "Gratitude can transform common days into thanksgiving, turn routine jobs into joy, and change ordinary opportunities into blessings." And to quote

Zig Ziglar: "Gratitude is the healthiest of all human emotions."[12]

Zig wasn't the first person to come up with that. Cicero also mentioned gratitude as the "mother of all of human feelings." If you "express and feel gratitude, (you) have a higher volume of gray matter in the right inferior temporal gyrus."[13]

According to an article by Vu Le:[14]

1. In general, at least in the U.S., it's good to express gratitude from time to time. This is an excellent way to demonstrate your humanity, which will be increasingly vital as artificial intelligence takes over our world.
2. Texts, emails, phone calls, videos, voicemails, or verbal expressions by themselves are sufficient demonstrations of gratitude. We must stop this elitist notion that writing, especially handwriting, is somehow the morally superior form of communication. I mean, have you met many writers?

Being Altruistic Has Health Benefits

I work hard for social interaction. I grease the wheels with cards, clippings, and correspondence. What goes out must come back. In a National Public Radio article citing altruism as a stress reliever, Vanessa Rancaño researched positive and negative emotions and had this to say: "Researchers already knew that people who are generally inclined toward altruism tend to be happier and live longer than those who aren't. What [was] discovered is that whatever your baseline level of antipathy may be, hating people a little bit less for the day can make you feel better."[15]

Find Something Nice to Say

There is magic in using the right words to show someone you care. As early as junior high school, this became my most effective technique when I dared float a message to a crush who didn't know I existed. Swapping sentences, not kisses, was how I got to know a boy I liked. First, I'd ask him to be my pen pal. If he accepted, we'd be off to the races. After my (hopefully) stimulating witticisms, he'd be hooked—and some form of contact would continue at least for a while.

When I was older and became dreamy eyed about a boy, my dad's sole piece of advice was: "Find something nice to say." His theory was that everyone is insecure and that nobody minds being told they're terrific. Even if they're not all that great, make them feel that way. My father used flattery with the precision of a brain surgeon.

I tried. I'd search for a positive attribute—not always easy. My first attempts were pitiful. I'd compliment "Zack" on his "beautiful smile," seconds before being blinded by his "metal-mouth." As a perpetual people pleaser, I would pump up the other person. I came on too strong and learned the hard way *not* to blurt out the first thing that came to mind. I got better at the concept of "zip it." (Years later, I heard a phrase from Alcoholics Anonymous that I loved so much I had it written on a T-shirt: **W.A.I.T.** It stands for "**W**hy **A**m **I T**alking?")

After many embarrassing gaffes I learned what to do: *Be genuine.* (Thank you, Dale Carnegie.) I improved with practice. If my comment hit the mark and I'd sussed out what the boy really was proud of about himself, the object of my affection's cheeks slowly turned pink, or a shy grin played on his lips. When that happened, I felt fantastic. It was intoxicating to own the power of a compliment. I was happy.

Marisa Murrow, a talented painter who attended the Rhode Island School of Design, gives me credit for inspiring her to reach out to people. She asks herself, "What would Erica do?" Of course, she's the one who deserves full credit for putting herself out there. She adds flower petals, feathers, and handmade sketches to her cards, and now she's making perfect greeting cards from the paintings she creates.

You can never go wrong with kindness. It's good for your mental health. The Mental Health Foundation in the United Kingdom says kindness banishes stress, makes you feel better physically, and improves your emotional well-being. A random act of kindness can brighten

> The Mental Health Foundation in the United Kingdom says kindness banishes stress, makes you feel better physically, and improves your emotional well-being.

MARISA MURROW

Hi Erica!

Welcome back! It looks like RISD threw quite a festive celebration for our new President... So positive to see photos of everyone together, maskless smiles on faces, music and carefree merriment. This is a part of life we all need for our survival!

I took your advice and posted on our RISD Alumni page inquiring if anyone had been to Headlands. Several people enthusiastically commented and one person went there. She said it was her favorite residency.

Sometimes I think to myself, what would Erica do..... She would write that letter _and_ send it. She would show up for what she believes in. When I asked my cousin if she would go to the Open House and take photos she invited me to come up for a visit. As a result of the letter I wrote to the Director, I am flying to San Francisco for an art filled weekend and special family time (so sweet she asked me to stay a while ☺). Hoping this gesture brings me closer to relatives and flags my application
* Artist with significant dedication to her work

Love,
Marisa

Letter to
Mr. and Mrs.
Leonard Maltin.

May 18, 2022

Mr. and Mrs. Leonard + Alice Maltin

Dear Leonard and Alice,

For years I've heard about how you and Vin worked together at "Entertainment Tonight", Leonard, and Vin is very proud of his connection with you.

Of course, I'd seen your reviews and felt like I knew you in some way, but meeting in person was much more gratifying.

And Alice, I've decided you could have your own talk show! You tell a captivating story, peppered with clever comments and brilliant insights -- and Donelle Dadigan had said you're a great addition to any party, and she was certainly correct!

Diane Baker and I had plotted for weeks to get us all together, and I was well aware of the deep Hollywood history that ran through all of you. We could have taped a segment last night -- not sure what it would have called, but it would have been captivating!

Thank you for being such good sports about no easy parking and intermittent seating. You make strangers feel instantly comfortable, and your knowledge about the entertainment world added a meaningful dimension (and warmth) to the Museum experience. I hope to see both of you soon, and it was a fantastic afternoon!
Yours truly,

Erica Gerard Di Bona

your day. Below are my favorites from their list of "50 random acts of kindness you can do today":[16]

> #2: "Send a letter to a grandparent."
> #5: "Send someone a handwritten note."
> #16: "Tell someone you know that you are proud of them."
> #17: "Tell someone you know why you are thankful for them."
> #21: "Send an inspirational quote to a friend."
> #22: "Send an interesting article to a friend."
> #24: "Contact someone you haven't seen in a while and arrange to meet face to face."
> #38: "Give praise to your colleague for something they've done well."

The research isn't a surprise, as far as I'm concerned. I enjoy making someone's day brighter. When I'm feeling the worst about my fellow human—frustrated at selfish drivers or scared by overt hostility between political parties, enemy countries, or the "haves" and "have nots"—I go the other way. As the news gets worse, my morning routine is my life raft. After I've stumbled downstairs to infuse my first cup of coffee, I scan the morning paper (yes, hard copy in color soy ink on newsprint!) and look for articles, horoscopes, or cartoons that remind me of someone I love. When I stick an envelope in the outgoing mail, I exhale and feel ready for the day—and hope I've contributed a tiny bit to civility.

My favorite letters include those from a famous film critic, a hairdresser, a little boy, and my daughter (who wrote a tribute to a teacher who protected her).

Leonard Maltin is a leading film critic whose movie guide was published annually for years, so he has encyclopedic knowledge of hundreds upon hundreds of films. He and his lively wife, Alice Tlusty, herself a producer, are quick-witted dinner companions and can speak knowledgeably about almost anything.

> I enjoy making someone's day brighter. When I'm feeling the worst about my fellow human— frustrated at selfish drivers or scared by overt hostility between political parties, enemy countries, or the "haves" and "have nots"—I go the other way.

Vin hired Leonard to be the film reviewer on *Entertainment Tonight*, a role he relished for thirty years.

Hairdresser + happy hair = Peter Vandevelde. The curse of short hair is that I need a haircut every four weeks. Peter Vandevelde was my daughter Jamie's hairdresser, and when she went to college I slid into Peter's jammed calendar. He's so talented that clients fly in from Kansas and drive in from Santa Barbara, San Diego, Orange County, and all over the Southland to sit in his chair. I don't take his talent for granted and tell him so, often.

After a birthday party honoring Dame Jane Goodall (an English primatologist and

Erica Gerard Di Bona

Peter Van de Velde, hairdresser, Jeffrey Kara Salon

March 28, 2013

Dear Peter,

    I finally feel like I'm not stranded without a hairdresser who understands me. You were able to diagnose my problems (it sounds like a psychiatrist!), look at my picture, and translate what I've been missing into a haircut that works.

    Your background in architecture definitely informs your work. I could tell when you said one side was longer than the other, that's what I'd unconsciously thought & feared but not been able to put into words. You found the weak spots and turned them into strengths.

    I also appreciated your showing me how to work with it to maximize volume. I'm not very talented in that way, and all helpful hints (and product recommendations) are something I really appreciate & take seriously!

    Your staff is courteous and organized. You are a delight, as always, and for the first time since my hairdresser moved to New York, I know I have found my new style partner. Thank you.

Warmest wishes,

Erica Gerard Di Bona

Erica Gerard Di Bona

Letter to hairdresser Peter.

Dear Erica
thank you for
the mushroom
because
mushroom
are one ok
my favor
foods and
Evrything
you give me
makes me
feel like

Card from Daniel about mushrooms.

anthropologist) at the home of my close friend Denise Avchen and her late husband, Terry, the swag bag was a "grow your own mushrooms" kit. I gifted it to one of my young pen pals, Daniel, and to my delight he loved it.

A student's heartfelt message may motivate a hardworking teacher for months, if not years. When Jamie was being bullied by an anonymous hater who thrust menacing messages into our home mailbox, we told her fifth-grade teacher, who gave the class a stern warning. The bullying soon ceased. I encouraged my daughter to write Mrs. Marcus a Thank You note along with the usual gift card at the end of the school year.

A Double Thank You, or Twice as Nice

Don't kill me, but sometimes I've double-thanked someone. I've been known to affirm

Dan_iel

our in my house becaause it's always awesome

Jamie's letter to her teacher.

June 21, 2000

Dear Mrs. Landau,

Thank you; for all the times you stood up for me, were a shoulder to cry on when people said mean things, for being more than a teacher – a friend.

It was a pleasure being in your class. I loved your teaching techniques. They really helped me with my confidence to learn new things. When I walked into your class, I didn't like math at all. Now I LOVE it! When I walked into your class, I didn't like reading. Now I ADORE it! You taught me more than curriculum – you taught me how to be true to myself, and how not to believe someone if you don't think it's true.

You helped me with my problems with friends, and tried to make things better. I learned a lot in fifth grade. I hope I'll learn as much in sixth grade. I wish that you were one of my Middle School teachers. I think you prepared me and almost everyone how to get by in Middle School. I hope that I like all the teachers as much as I liked you.

I really loved being in your class. Thank you again.
Love,

Jamie Goldstein

---

twice in *two separate letters* sent *years apart* how much I continued to enjoy what they did or gave me. If your gift-getting happiness is retriggered, share it! For example, I told Lara, the interior designer who oversaw repainting and updating our kitchen during COVID-19, how every time I walk in the room and see its sage-colored cabinets and white marble granite countertop, I smile all over again, even three years later.

What are the odds I'm the only client ever to write her twice?

A "Thanks to Me" Letter

Many of us are our own worst critics. I've always been punishing of myself. It dates back to when I was three or four and would hit my hand repeatedly, saying, "Bad hand, bad hand," until it stung too much and I would stop. In Co-

> A personal letter is a portal to the past. It takes both you and your recipient back to another time and allows you to bask in your memory of what happened then.

Dependents Anonymous and Alcoholics Anonymous, which I have been a member of for decades now, you're supposed to forgive *yourself* before you ask others whom you hurt for their absolution. I'm just now learning to treat myself with kid gloves, and I'm ashamed to say it's taken me the majority of my life to cleanse myself of sins that only I see as problematic or "less than."

An "I Apologize to Me" Letter

Harriet Hunter writes in *Miracles of Recovery: Daily Meditations of Hope, Courage and Faith* that there are many ways to apologize to oneself. You might carve out a quiet hour or so to think about ways you have hurt your own feelings and then list the ways you can thank yourself. Here I offer a truncated version of Harriet's advice:[17]

- I am doing the best I can—and so is everyone else. *Thank you for being you.*
- I deserve *my* understanding, compassion, and forgiveness. *Thank you for forgiving yourself.*
- I love you (your name) as you are. *Thank you for being you.*
- I no longer need to feel berated, put down, or less than. *Thank you for being enough today.*
- I know, accept, and am true to myself. *Thank you for being true to myself.*
- I believe in, trust, and have confidence in myself. *Thank you for trusting myself.*
- I deserve to take care of my physical, psychological and emotional self. *Thank you for taking good care of my well-being.*
- I know I can accomplish anything I set my mind to. *Thank you for being strong and persistent.*
- I am not perfect, and I'm grateful. I am a spiritual being having a human experience of imperfection, and that's okay. *Thank you for being perfectly imperfect.*

I owe myself multiple apologies and thank yous. I'm consciously not tracing back to my childhood because those mistakes, missteps, and misunderstandings are too numerous to count, and I blame my attention-deficit disorder for causing my poor decision-making and impulsive bad choices. My fractured sense of self-worth has taken years to buttress, and I'm just now starting to feel that it's my time.

I didn't need nasty bosses to excoriate me because I could make myself feel terrible without much effort. During my TV career, I continued to be my own harshest critic. When my production job entailed a brutal commute, endless to-do lists spun in my head as I lurched along the choked-up freeway.

To multitask and keep from going crazy, I'd leave a reminder on my answering machine (remember those?) of what I needed to do, fix, bring to work, etc. The message was hasty and gruff, in a drill sergeant tone, like, "Do *this*!" and "Don't forget *that*!" I was shocked at how fierce I sounded when I replayed it. My daughter Jamie was in elementary school and would be doing her homework as these vile, authoritative orders clouded the kitchen. They were harsh, punitive, and scary. She would look frightened, and I would feel ashamed. I wouldn't talk to *her* that way, so why did I do it to myself? As a parent trying to imprint how to become a loving adult on her, I was doing a terrible disservice to both of us.

I consciously turned over a new leaf. I changed my tone, softened my voice, and added a sign-off: "I love you, Erica." It changed the whole dynamic. Now my reminders make me feel warm and loved—by myself! I also thank myself for being productive and efficient or allowing myself to cancel a plan or not do a task if I feel tired.

Thoughtful Connections That Save Time

Another benefit of sending letters is that it's a way to be kind without going overboard. If I don't have a lot of time to chat on the phone or start an endless text chain, I let a letter do the talking. This is efficient because I don't have to engage with the recipients on *their* schedule—I can connect when I'm in the right mindset. My outreach can even occur at midnight, when some of my best work happens.

Letter writing acts like its own form of meditation and reflection. You slow down and immerse yourself in contemplating what you want to say. It's the slow cookery of connection. You can remind yourself of a good experience as you share it. The act of corresponding may

release serotonin, which combats depression—another reason to capture your thoughts on paper. If you are a scribe, life won't pass you by. When you recapture all the excitement and glory in words, your world becomes Technicolor instead of black and white. You capture the story and make it indelible. It lingers.

It also maintains that happy high. Writing a letter after an event compliments the host on all the warm and fuzzy feelings their party gave you. And ninety-nine times out of a hundred, I am the only one doing a follow-up (and, in my case, typing it!), so that action alone imprints on their mind.

This morning my friend Sal Viscuso texted me a picture of a thank you note I'd written him fifteen years ago after he'd made fresh pasta—

> Letter writing acts like its own form of meditation and reflection. You slow down and immerse yourself in contemplating what you want to say. It's the slow cookery of connection.

fed through his own pasta machine and sun-warmed on the drying rack in our courtyard—and pine-nut-studded beef braciole for Vin and me. He'd kept the note all this time, which speaks to the staying power of a card. Seeing my words again reminded me of Sal's culinary lesson of love.

A personal letter is a portal to the past. It takes both you and your recipient back to another time and allows you to bask in your memory of what happened then. Think about a bride and groom who request a contribution to their honeymoon to Africa as a wedding gift. Wouldn't it be delightful to receive a card a year later with a buoyant montage of pictures of the two newlyweds in the Sahara? The couple shares the adventure again, creating their own photographic cards of animals they saw and places they went, and their guests symbolically join them on their honeymoon. (Technically, wedding etiquette states the new couple is allowed *three months* from the date they received the gift to generate Thank Yous. If you're the guest, relax—you have up to a year to buy them something.)

If you start with the premise "find something nice to say," you have an immediate head start on cranking out a meaningful piece of prose in your Thank You. The exchanges I've included here—such as where I thank a film critic and his wife after a fascinating evening or tell my hairdresser he's like God with a pair of scissors—brought happiness to all of us and took me very little time to execute.

The twelve-step program of Alcoholics Anonymous and Co-Dependents Anonymous taught me that while I was so busy looking out for everybody else, I was failing to be kind to myself and find my own happiness. There's something bubbly and wonderful about finding something nice to say about yourself. It feels a little naughty and self-serving (if you're not a narcissist who's used to praising yourself).

Letter writing is also a way to claim more free time if you opt to write a quick note instead of spending an hour gabbing on the phone to a talkative friend. Letters are a time-stamped keepsake from the past, a reminder of who we are now and who we aspire to be. Just as we say music is the soundtrack to our lives, a letter is a time capsule that seals a moment in history—a time of self-examination and declaration. Later, when we're feeling depressed or insecure, it gives us a drawer to rifle through to find something nice to tell ourselves, such as a message from a friend or family member sent just to say, "I love you." ●

> If you start with the premise "find something nice to say," you have an immediate head start on cranking out a meaningful piece of prose in your Thank You.

Typewriter key necklace gifted
to Erica by Doris Nemtzow.

Erica wearing the typewriter
key necklace in this photo,
seated with Jane Goodall.

Chapter Four

Thank People for the Little Stuff

We all want a happy life, a great job, a functional family (as opposed to dysfunctional!), money in the bank, and friends. Oh, and I almost forgot good health.

It's hard to grasp at the idea of having everything, but maybe you have more bandwidth in your existence than you realize. Do you take stock of what you have very often? One way to appreciate what's already in front of us is this simple concept I coined: "Thanks for being you." It's low tech and high impact. The idea is hardly complex, and doesn't require any kind of degree, but by thanking people with a letter or card for what they have done to enhance your world, you spotlight the best parts of the way you live. I encourage you to add "thanks for being you" to your tool kit; I promise I will further explain how to incorporate it in your life.

In the last ten years I've become proactive in taking time to compose a "thanks for being you" note. In fundraising, I've found this message has the same connecting effect with future donors as it does with vendors and other professionals. It puts me squarely on their radar. If a typed letter has preceded me, they will remember me when I call or reach out again (and the typewriter format is memorable in and of itself). It makes *them* feel good to see that I took the time to handcraft a message—and their satisfied reaction makes me happy too.

It's a tiny love letter disguised in a Thank You.

I write different kinds of "thanks for being you" letters depending on the circumstances: from Ignacio, who hauls our garbage out at dawn, to Danny the tailor, who's able to salvage a dress perfectly, to museum directors, entertainment titans, doctors, and salespeople. That's how I let people know I see and appreciate them.

I'll track down the theater office to write a congrats to an actor on a wonderful stage performance. I've sent letters to former bosses thanking them for what they taught me; to a local deli owner for donating lox and bagels for a fundraiser; and after a leisurely Sunday brunch (with plenty of mimosas), thanking the manager of the jazz bar.

Once, when my daughter admired a table crumb sweeper at a steak restaurant, I wrote a letter to the kind waiter who spontaneously presented it to her.

One way to appreciate what's already in front of us is this simple concept I coined: "Thanks for being you." It's low tech and high impact.

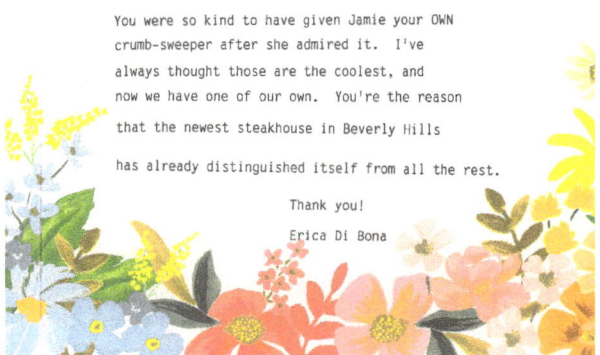

You were so kind to have given Jamie your OWN crumb-sweeper after she admired it. I've always thought those are the coolest, and now we have one of our own. You're the reason that the newest steakhouse in Beverly Hills has already distinguished itself from all the rest.

Thank you!
Erica Di Bona

Letter from Erica to the server who gifted the crumb sweeper.

I don't hesitate to praise the friendly owner of our favorite Italian restaurant either. There's a direct line between letting a merchant know they've done a fantastic job and how quickly that businessperson then wants to get your project on their calendar. When I show appreciation in a letter to the service professionals who repair the broken washer, refrigerator, or patio at my house, I notice their responsiveness goes up a thousand percent. Whether it's replacing a broken water heater or cleaning carpets after an exuberant partygoer spills red wine, I'm pretty sure I get pushed higher on the priority list.

We can also write Thank Yous in admiration of another person's talents and gifts, like when your mentor takes you to lunch to discuss your next career move. Or when your girlfriend, a wannabe fashion stylist, drives you to the mall to unearth that elusive mother-of-the-bride dress with floaty sleeves to hide aging arms. Or when your buddy moves your refrigerator and only requests a beer and pizza for his efforts. They have given generously of their "time, talent, and treasure." The least you can do in return is send them a Thank You!

Six Broken Ribs and Star Service

My plumber Fred Morrow performed a miracle despite six broken ribs and more than deserved a "thanks for being you" letter. We had a flood in the basement, and his staff was out sick, so as the owner, he came over and saved the day. Only later did I learn he'd been so compromised. To me that was the mark of a true professional.

Lots of Smog

I live in a busy city, where cars and smog are as damaging to cleanliness (and clear lungs) as the natural elements. My house windows attract dust and dirt at an alarming rate, but our window washer, Oscar, is up to the task twelve months a year. Often I wait until the rains are over to schedule him, but this particular spring I procrastinated too long. It was the hottest day of the year when he appeared. I felt guilty watching him clamber up ladders, sweating profusely, bucket in hand. I tucked a message in with the check. The money was the point, but a few nice words added to the sweetness of the envelope.

The Henna Tattoo

In addition to roasted turkey drumsticks and deep-fried Oreos, the Orange County Fair features 150 experiences, including feeding baby animals, ogling crazy inventions, and getting a henna tattoo. When Vin's teenaged granddaughters wanted temporary insignia, they encouraged me to try it too. I hesitantly found a sign for "strength," and Omar the artist set me at ease by asking questions as he drew.

I shared my belief in Thank Yous and we had a lovely conversation. I then sent him my form of writing. Months later, he called. He'd filed the letter away and just found it again. After a painful breakup, he was in emotional hell, but my note renewed his faith in people. He declared no customer had ever been that kind. (And there are 4.3 million visitors a year to that venue!) He hoped I would visit the fair again and offered free tickets. I never made it but appreciated his invitation.

My Man in Blue and the Blue Box

True confession: I had a crush on my wonderful postman Tim Shackelford. As handsome as any movie star, he appeared every weekday afternoon in his starched blue uniform, handing me a pile of papers with a big smile. I made "beat the postman" a game, rushing to place a letter in the mailbox seconds before he got there. He enjoyed my productivity, and I kept him busy with my output. He assured me nobody else on his route sent out as many packages and envelopes.

When my father died, Tim the mailman spotted the blue box of cremated remains when it arrived at my house. (Side note: The only organization authorized to send ashes of a dead person is USPS. Federal Express and United Parcel Service don't deal with them.) Last thing Tim knew was that I was up north visiting my father. He didn't know my dad

Erica Gerard Di Bona

August 8, 2012

Mr. Fred Morrow

Dear Fred:

Gregory McAllester told me about what a true professional you were yesterday -- how you showed up at my house on La Peer, because your staff was all out sick, and even though you'd broken six ribs you still jumped in to move the water heater...tromp down the narrow stairs to the flooded basement, and fix the problem.

Vin and I are very grateful to know that you are a person who goves ABOVE AND BEYOND. You are there for us in emergency times. You have your "A team" available to fix pesky problems. And your staff is always pleasant and quick-witted when we call, day or night.

Thank you for coming to our rescue -- not only yesterday at La Peer, but over and over again in so many situations. We hope you heal quickly, and if good deeds count toward medical miracles -- you should hope to shave off a few weeks of recovery time in exchange for what you did for us yesterday.

Best,

Erica & Vin Di Bona

Erica Gerard Di Bona

June 28, 2013

Dear Oscar --

Thank you for washing our windows on what was the hottest day of the new summer.

We appreciate being able to see out more clearly, and will think of you each time we appreciate the clear view.

Best,

Erica & Vin Di Bona

9023
16-1606/1220
669

Date

$

Dollars

Gerard Di Bona

September 9, 2015

Mr. Omar Qureshi
Director of Operations/
Advanced Artist
Creative Henna

Dear Omar:

It was a few weeks ago -- almost a month or so, really -- when I summoned up the courage to allow you to show off your artistic skills on my ankle.

I was hesitant. I've never done a henna tattoo, or any tattoo at all -- and I didn't want to live with something that I wouldn't enjoy looking at for the next few days.

Much to my delight, you were able to allay my concerns... and draw free-hand the symbol of "strength" that I had chosen. You added a few dollops of sprinkle afterwards, and kept me engaged in conversation about my 'thank you' notes as we worked together on your creation.

Your company was very well-run and I appreciated that you took your time, cared about each customer, and whether we were old pros at doing it -- or first-timers like me -- you made each of us feel comfortable.

I would recommend CREATIVE HENNA to any organization, and most importantly, I would say, "Make sure you get Omar -- he's terrific."

Best,

Erica Gerard Di Bona
Customer at Orange County Fair

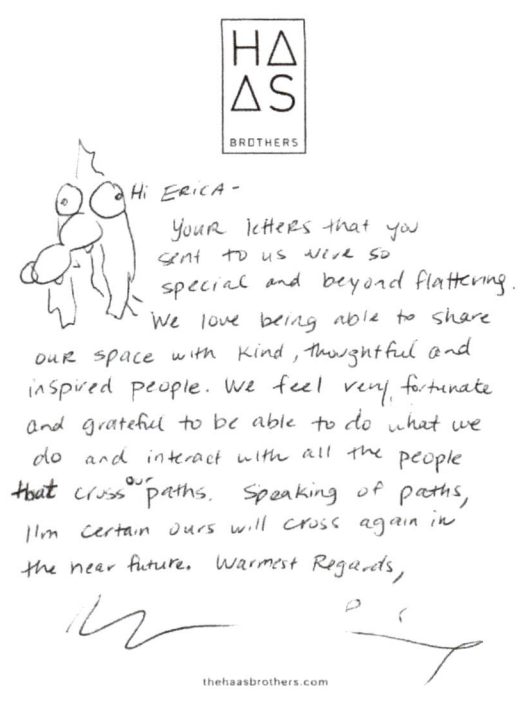

HAAS
BROTHERS

Hi ERICA –

Your letters that you
sent to us were so
special and beyond flattering.
We love being able to share
our space with kind, thoughtful and
inspired people. We feel very fortunate
and grateful to be able to do what we
do and interact with all the people
that cross our paths. Speaking of paths,
I'm certain ours will cross again in
the near future. Warmest Regards,

thehaasbrothers.com

Card from the Haas brothers.

was gone because he hadn't seen me since it happened.

Postman Tim figured it out from my decreased outgoing mail: No more letters headed to Gary Gerard at 2 Anchor Drive. My mailman personally signed for the navy blue box, as it required a next of kin signature or it would be sent back to the post office. When I got home, I hastened into the courtyard to tell Tim the sad news—but he beat me to it.

"I'm sorry about your loss," he said, before I'd even opened my mouth. "When I saw the blue box ... I didn't want your Dad going back to the post office."

After Tim retired, Vin and I treated him and his "lady friend" to dinner. I still send Tim notes when I think he'd be interested in some piece of news. My new mail lady is pleasant, but it's not the same.

Stationery Doodles

Fraternal twins Nikolai and Simon Haas create otherworldly sculptures and furniture that merge art and design, showcasing fur, gold, and ceramics. Only Simon attended Rhode Island School of Design, but both brothers are great admirers of the institution and have opened their Los Angeles studios on numerous occasions to events for parents and students. After one such evening, I praised their hospitality and expansive hearts—and they responded. Their official notepaper was so cool, and their pencil drawing pleased me. I felt I was in the presence of artists. I especially loved the little design of a face with glasses on a big nose (top left). We have corresponded several times, and it's set the tone for a warm connection.

Strengthening Bonds Despite the Distance

Since the COVID-19 pandemic, many of us now work at home and rarely meet our coworkers face-to-face. To deepen the long-distance relationship, I send Thank You notes to colleagues even if I've not yet met them in real life. It's a challenge to get to know a teammate in a different city. Letters pave the way, and they've helped me make better friends with Samantha, the Chief of Staff who coordinates meetings with my boss the Vice Chancellor, or I formally compliment (in a letter) the head of Career Services after she's downloaded internship information for me.

When University of California, Santa Cruz IT expert Jeff tried to get me technically proficient on my university-issued laptop—and I'd had multiple meltdowns—I sent him a box of See's Candies after our shared ordeal to let him know I *really* appreciated his patience. He confessed that the chocolate bridge mix was nice but that the note would last longer. (Zero calories too!)

If you're in a meeting or on a Zoom call where someone of influence makes a stirring point, creates a winning phrase, or pushes past the ordinary, write a mini fan letter to them. Especially in the age of disembodied phone calls where we are no longer in the same room, it's got to be rewarding to be told, "I loved what you said." I've never met anyone who doesn't appreciate a pat on the back. (Well, maybe one.) If they *do* have a problem or it would be too much of a kiss-up, don't bother. But nine times out of ten, with a few kind words, you'll vault yourself to the top of the class.

Jon Kamen: An Innovator

Jon Kamen creates content for feature films, Academy Award-nominated documentaries, commercials, music, graphic and interactive designs, exhibitions, and photography. His company revamped the *My Next Guest Needs No Introduction* series with David Letterman; he even has a picture of himself standing between Barack (Obama) and Dave (Letterman). Radical Media delivers surprising stories, from that of the depraved pedophiliac sex offender Jeffrey Epstein to that of the delightful Lin-Manuel Miranda (*Hamilton*) to *Summer of Soul*.

Jon was a trustee for Rhode Island School of Design. He is passionate and high energy when he bounds into a room, iPad in hand, sporting chartreuse-striped running shoes and ready for

action. When Jon's "on fire," he spins a topic until he arrives at a conclusion so stunning and high concept that we all wish we had thought of it.

At one board meeting, watery sunshine pelted the windows as we sat under artwork created by talented students. Jon launched into his innovative way to solve a knotty problem. When Jon Kamen "sets the bar high," I applaud. If I'm his wingman, so be it. There are worse things, and I'm honored to have been in the same room as him. After the board meeting, I wrote to him about how much I admired his great ideas, and he wrote me back.

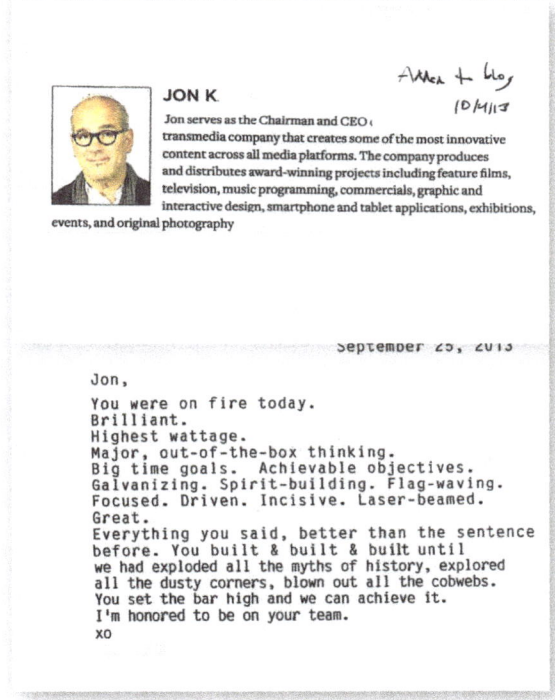

Letter to Jon Kamen.

Erica —

You are the gift

that keeps on giving.
You're not only a great
wingman, but a great friend.

Love you —

J

Note from
Jon Kamen.

Sometimes a Message We Write May Be the Last

I met my college roommate Karen Schmidt's younger sister Joel when I was eighteen. She had a broad gap-toothed smile and gazed up at me with unconditional love (she wasn't very tall). She lived with gusto: She invariably picked the item on the menu with the most calories and would devour her gooey banana split while Karen and I unhappily poked away at our more sensible salads.

Joel was born on December 25, and her family celebrated her birthday as the top priority, then held Christmas at night. She was the first person I knew with Down syndrome.

Joel watched network news and was a proud Democrat. She wore her "I voted" sticker like the Hope Diamond. She loved television, and her favorite programs inevitably were top-rated. My former husband Josh, a TV producer, would quiz her: "Joel, what are you watching? *Why* do you like it?" He was trying to divine the secret code for a hit show. She was eerily accurate when it came to the best TV—*Gilmore Girls* was a favorite.

Many years ago I threw a Hanukkah party and invited Karen, her husband, Roger, and Joel. Our house was decked for Christmas *and* the eight days of Hanukkah (Vin is Catholic and I'm Jewish). Joel was wide-eyed at our highly decorated tree. At the white elephant exchange, she won a white fedora, which she promptly donned, and a Mickey Mouse waffle maker, which she hugged to her chest. We all ate frosted cookies and smashed gingerbread houses with a meat mallet—don't ask. Brisket and latkes first, then an ice cream sundae buffet. Joel was first in line, peppermint-striped bowl in hand.

And she was the last to leave. She stood on tiptoe to hug me and breathed in my ear, "I *loved* it!"

Later I received a darling card from the party girl. Karen, older sister and always the professional editor, inserted a word, but it was Joel's printing. My heart swelled when I saw her effort, and I wrote her back. I'm glad I did.

A few months later, Joel died in her sleep. A blessing, we decided. Joel reached "double nickels"—fifty-five—but not much longer. At the memorial, her special needs friends grieved loudly. A bright spark was gone. We all felt the loss.

Recently I was rifling through my desk, and in a stack of supposedly blank cards, one had familiar loopy large script on it: Joel's Thank You for the night she was a star. Joel touched my heart. When I see her distinctive scrawl, I feel her love. And isn't that what a letter should do?

Flirty and Dirty

Speaking of love, there are other kinds of love, like the X-rated kind. What about the thank you for a gratifying evening (wink-wink)?

In this day and age, odds are you are not going to send a letter to thank someone for a great night of sex. You might rip off a text, which is fun, fast, and easy. (I'm not going to discuss risqué videos featuring private parts; figure those out on your own if you're old enough.) This is another example of where *a letter is better.*

If you're trying to flirt, it's easy to send a text message embedded with a suggestive emoji, but a purple eggplant is not the same as hot words on the page. Plus, you can't keep a copy of it forever unless you did a screenshot, and then what?

In an effort to better understand what younger people are doing to send sexy texts, I went down a sex emoji rabbit hole. Here is what I found: The red heart emoji is the classic expression of love and romance. All long, phallic-shaped emojis represent a penis, including the eggplant, hot dog, banana, carrot, baguette, snake, and even rooster. A peace sign means vagina, the peach emoji means butt, and so on.

Let's get back on track: A letter can land in someone's lap when they need it the most. It may help them through a vulnerable time, after a breakup, or when they feel depressed and alone. It can serve as a reminder of an artist's talent, whether they are a museum-quality sculptor or a tattoo artist at the fair. It can laud a talented colleague who is always the first to turn a phrase, create a campaign, and rally the troops. It can remind a public servant how much they mean to society or highlight a hardworking contractor who goes above and beyond the call of duty. It can be the last letter you open from a special friend, although you won't know it at the time.

Or on a happier note, instead of an emoji-laden sexy text, it can be the secret, on-fire letter you sent that shows up years later in a deposition (!) or gets stashed away under your boyfriend's bed. There are as many formats as there are words. Whatever you decide to write will embed itself in your recipient's heart if you choose your phrases carefully, and you will make an impact that lives on far past the day you produced it. ●

Typewriter-themed jewelry and a typewriter key bracelet from Erica's collection.

Dial Typewriter toy
from the 1920s.

Chapter Five

Young People Thank Yous

Why is it such a tough sell to get "young people" (spanning from kindergarten to age thirty) to write Thank Yous? In my conversations with ninth graders and college students preparing to graduate, I've discovered one primary fear: They believe they don't have the skill or capability to write a good thank you letter, and unless a parent, grandparent, or teacher shows them how to do it, they have no idea where to start. One high school girl that I talked to was the only student in the entire class who received a piece of snail mail, and that turned out to be a postcard appointment reminder from her dentist. Millennials[18] and Gen Zers worry that endearing themselves to people in higher positions of authority makes their outreach appear disingenuous. They're concerned they will be perceived as manipulative if they "game the system" by sending a note of appreciation after an interview. I'm stunned by that fear, as it has never occurred to me!

Now add in the worry about being manipulative to the corrosive mixture of (1) not knowing or practicing good penmanship, (2) not having a backstock of paper products or pens nearby, (3) not knowing where to buy stamps (or how much they cost), (4) not knowing how many stamps to affix to the envelope, and (5) not knowing where to mail it. The process is intimidating.

The Thank You note is a dying art, and it's our responsibility as "elders" to impress its importance on the younger set, who have a tendency for self-absorption. When you show your offspring how to send brief letters and think of someone other than themselves, you're helping them develop a social skills "muscle" that improves their empathy. If the younger generation learns how meaningful an outreach can be when their friend is happy or sad, you're also teaching them about altruism and compassion. You're allowing them to extend their heart and care about *other* people's feelings.

I once went to Berkeley, California, for what was supposed to be a few days to help my dad after knee surgery. Two weeks later, after nervously guarding his safety 24/7 and making sure he had pain meds and did his required physical therapy, I headed home. I was exhausted but happy to have been there for him.

On the airplane, as I downed a complimentary gin and tonic—my usual reward after another debilitating parental trip—and ordered a second watered-down drink, it occurred to me: If I was sick, would my teenage daughter Jamie do the same for me? I knew the answer.

It was time for a little lecture.

When my daughter and I got together, I broached the subject. "Jamie, after being with Grandpa this week, I wasn't sure that if I ever get really sick, you would look out for me the same way I did for Grandpa. I think we need to work on your empathy."

She blinked and innocently and unironically asked, "What's empathy?"

I tried not to laugh because I had hit the nail on the head. My examples were sixth-grader appropriate: "It's caring about someone before you think about yourself. It's sending a birthday

> The Thank You note is a dying art, and it's our responsibility as "elders" to impress its importance on the younger set, who have a tendency for self-absorption.

card even though you don't **like cards yourself** but your friend does, so you let your friend know you love them and are thinking of them. It's making someone feel special by wondering, 'What would it feel like to be that person?' It's learning how to put yourself in someone else's shoes."

Jamie was losing interest, and I decided "'nuff said," as my Granddaddy Al muttered when a discussion was over. But I made a mental note to circle back later—and you can bet I did!

Never Too Young to Start

It's never too early to start encouraging gratitude. I started letter writing young, probably around first grade, with my grandfather. He lived in Seattle, Washington, and we

> What's fascinating is that in every piece of mail, their ability to express themselves increases, and their vocabulary expands.

corresponded **every** week. He was a retiree, and life was quiet. He reported little stuff, like his jaunt to Pike Place Market to find fresh Dungeness crab paired with coleslaw and sourdough bread. He described moments of his routine so that I could virtually walk alongside him, sharing the ups and downs of his life. Thanks to his colorful narratives, I felt closer despite the physical distance. It was our own FaceTime, without faces.

Ever since those interactions with my grandfather, I've wanted other children to feel joy when they spy a letter in the mailbox. I've introduced tiny toddlers as young as four to the rush of writing (or scribbling, as it may be). What's fascinating is that in every piece of mail, their ability to express themselves increases, and their vocabulary expands. As they become familiar with the concept of sharing what's going on, they write longer sentences. As they get older, they level up to recounting what they did that day or what they learned in school. When their messages feature more

words and fewer pictures, I interpret that as growth and secretly celebrate their linguistic development. We can parlay this joy of letters into thanking others.

If you're part of my generation—called "Boomers" because of the post-war baby boom—we complain how we don't get letters from our children or grandchildren, but we don't try to fix it. We Boomers were born anywhere from 1946, right after World War II, to 1964—the result of the mid-twentieth-century baby boom. Our parents were part of the Greatest Generation or the Silent Generation. (Millennials have the biggest demographic, followed by Boomers, who come in second.) When Boomers were growing up the only way to contact someone was by writing a letter or making a phone call (and dialing long-distance on a rotary phone or calling "collect" from a phone booth, which was expensive!).

We should set a good example when we ask younger generations to send us snail mail. Children are comfortable with FaceTime, which is fast and immediate, based on impulse with no forethought. Meanwhile, snail mail letters take days to arrive (hence the term!), so we should teach kids they need to have patience both to formulate a letter and then to wait for an answer.

Grandparents, I'm reminding you here that even when we initiate contact, we give up after a while if the kids don't reply. Some grandparents will send pre-stamped letters and be dismayed (and sometimes angered, if radio silence continues) that their grandchildren totally blew them off. We feel disregarded, and our grandchildren can't understand the problem. Plus, what is the kid's incentive? We are all built on incentives. I use bribes of candy and money for my pen pals or grandkids, or if it's a camp or college situation, I curate a box full of nonperishable food. (Manchego cheese, found at Costco, travels well without refrigeration. Beef jerky, a whole salami, microwave popcorn, breakfast or protein bars, peanut butter, and crackers are also solid choices.) I announce I won't send anything more until I've gotten a response for the first package. I try to remain playful and fun, but the kids know I'm dead serious.

I'll confess, I'm not above bribing my youthful correspondents—it's a hundred percent guarantee they'll turn around a speedy Thank You if they know they'll get a shipment of chocolate or Haribo gummies or Sour Patch chewy candy (watermelon and peach seem to be favorites).

When I drag myself home after a particularly tedious slog and spy an envelope from one of my earnest pen pals, a big smile lights up my face. One envelope received from a tiny correspondent nullifies doctors' invoices and nasty MasterCard and utility bills. My newly indoctrinated reporter feels good for doing their outreach, and we, the elders, are happy they did, so the energetic flow of the Thank You is in place—similar to the "thank you for being you." We are just ensuring the art of Thank You doesn't die in the younger generations.

When my daughter Jamie was in college at Rhode Island School of Design, she was across the country from her family in California. My father, her Grandpa Gary, was a big believer that she'd make new friends more quickly if word got out that she kept fresh food in her tiny bar-sized dorm refrigerator. He lovingly packaged up Manchego cheese and Lindt dark chocolate bars and threw in a few tins of sardines for good measure, as he considered those the perfect solution for hungry kids with no cold storage. He told me canned protein never goes bad. He figured the more perishable items would last in the FedEx box for a few days if she didn't immediately

retrieve them from the school's mailroom and the weather wasn't too hot.

"Don't get your feelings hurt if you don't hear from her," I warned my dad. I explained that she was busy and that even I rarely got a buzz, except sometimes when she was between

I'll confess, I'm not above bribing my youthful correspondents—it's a hundred percent guarantee they'll turn around a speedy Thank You if they know they'll get a shipment of chocolate or Haribo gummies or Sour Patch chewy candy (watermelon and peach seem to be favorites).

classes and walking to the dining hall or late at night after she'd been painting in her studio.

My father immediately decided a hurried phone call wasn't good enough and he wouldn't go to such trouble if he didn't get a grateful response in a timely fashion. He devised the perfect strategy to goad her into gratitude. He'd warn: "Jamie, dear girl, call me after you get this package, or I won't send another one." Bingo! She'd check in within hours of receiving the box, and Grandpa Gary was the *only* person throughout her college career who had that power over her.

Trust me, you *do* have the power here. Send food if you want to hear from a kid and want instant results. Beware that chocolate doesn't survive super-hot weather, though. Even so, I recommend the two most important foods in the "ch" category: cheese and chocolate! Sardines are another story.

There is also the money bribe, but many kids don't use cash or have checking accounts, and envelopes bearing cash are not safe from mail thieves anymore, so find alternative methods. But receiving Venmo, PayPal, Cash App, or Zelle money infusions will never be the same as slitting open an envelope and having fresh green dollar bills fall into your hand.

Letter writing expands personal growth.

The Times of Technology

It's truly not the kids' fault that they don't write letters. Times have changed with texting and social media DMs (a DM is a private, personal, or direct message only viewable by the participants. "Sliding into someone's DMs" means making the first move to initiate a conversation with someone because they found your profile appealing. It usually has flirtatious connotations, like buying someone a drink from across the room to get their attention).

"Sexting" means sending, receiving, or forwarding sexually explicit messages, videos, and photos, usually between mobile phones. But there is a risk of sending sexts and the receiver then sending them on to someone else. Statistics say that one in four teens are *receiving* sexually explicit texts and emails, while one in seven are *sending* sexts. Many of those are forwarded without the original sender's knowledge, and the originator *certainly* didn't grant permission for other prying eyes to see their "for your eyes only" sext. In that murky territory is where cyberbullying begins.[19]

This makes a wonderful argument for teaching young people to send letters with some sexy words, minus the pictures.

Catch this irony: More kids can create and send dirty emojis than know how to decipher longhand. The days of children being required to learn cursive are gone.[20] Handwriting was actually dying out at one point (in 2016, when only fourteen states taught cursive) but had a resurgence, so now twenty-one states require kids to learn cursive (as of 2018–2019). But think it through: If kids are not learning how to write cursive, how can they read it?

Therefore, if you want to send a letter to a college kid, do the following:

1. **Type it.** Otherwise they may not know how to read the longhand.

2. **Confirm** they have found their campus mailbox and make sure they check it once in a while. You may have sent them something, but they'll have no idea it's sitting there because visiting the mailbox on any regular kind of schedule is utterly foreign to them.

3. **Be persistent and consistent.** I've written my grandson Sam at college every week and made peace with the fact that although I don't get a reply in kind, he'll sometimes call or text to let me know he appreciates the letters and to keep them coming. (Every month or so I'll include a box of See's Bridge Mix chocolate to get his attention too.) Your effort will not fall on deaf ears. One day I might even get a letter back from him, but I'm not betting on it.

Why It's Important to Teach Younger Generations to Write

Letter writing expands personal growth. Much like crafting a school essay, committing words to paper helps one develop their own voice and vocabulary, express their emotions, and clarify their ideas. When a younger person knows they can write you with an open heart, without receiving judgment or correction, you give them a safe place to land. They will learn to organize their thoughts in a way that makes sense.

I once had a stretch class with a beautiful single mom named Ieva who told me about her young son, Daniel. As a single, divorced mom, too, I related to her challenges and began bringing notes to my session for her to bring home to Daniel. Much to my surprise—and delight—he wanted to write back, and soon Ieva and I were handling correspondence and candy (me) with notes in return (Daniel).

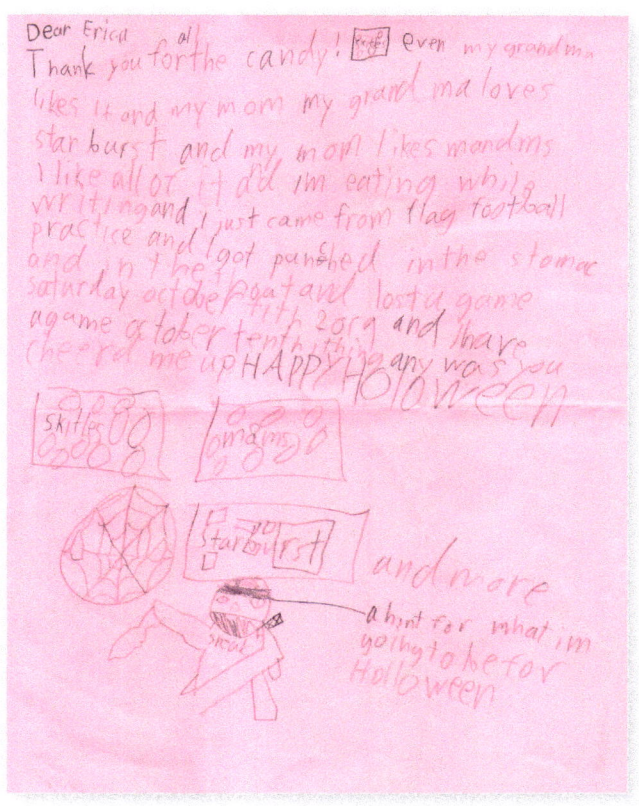

Thank you note for the candy from Daniel.

We still hadn't met, so we arranged to have ice cream together and talk. A while later, Ieva moved away from the area because she'd gotten engaged to a wonderful man. I continued my correspondence with Daniel, and he's now a teenager. Once I didn't have any candy to send, so I enclosed a $20 bill—which he appreciated and said would use it to buy candy for his friends. We've still only met that one time. I keep feeling I should drive out to where they live now and see who that eager young boy has become.

Letter writing imparts social skills and presumes a two-way conversation designed to elicit a response from the young receiver.

It prepares them to be better students and people. As they get older, these social skills will help them interact more genuinely with others, whether they are trying to make a positive impression or convince someone to fall in love with them!

The Letter Writing Toolbox Incentive

Your target audience for the great letter writing insurgence is not willing at all. They likely have no or a very limited attention span and definitely no accessible writing implements. Many kids sit at the busy kitchen table or lounge on the sofa with their iPhone within reach, so they're not using a classic office desk. (During the COVID-19 pandemic, when classroom schooling moved home, a dedicated desk was a vital piece of furniture many people had to buy, scrounge, or make from scratch for their kids. Many a kitchen counter or dining room table was pressed into service.)

Proper lighting is helpful, so you can see what you're doing, as is a stable writing surface. A desk needs accessories, such as a stapler, staple remover, tape dispenser, scissors, Post-its, pen and paper—because who uses those anymore and has them on hand? When young Daniel became my pen pal, his mother shared that he immediately sat down at his little desk and straightened all the papers on it. When he was done, he carefully stored previous correspondence in the drawer. That showed great executive function for a four-year-old. I loved that image!

There's a world of office supplies you can introduce your child to as well. Maybe organize a trip to the office supply store or find the stationery section at an art supply store. Upscale, trend-forward stores with general merchandise have a good cross-section of items too. Show your new writer where to affix stickers to the letter itself to close the back of the envelope. Buy some washi tape, a special Japanese decorative tape made of rice paper and used in craft projects such as scrapbooking. It is often called "Japanese masking tape"—although I don't know why since it doesn't adhere that well. The product comes in all sorts of colors and designs.

You want to make it easy and *fun* for your budding correspondents to send something back, so assume they are *not* working at a desk with every implement they need. Start with first things first. Remember, we were probably taught by our parents, grandparents, or elementary school teachers how to compose and dispatch a letter, but this activity is a thing of the past that we're trying to revive. You should assume *none* of the process is familiar to them.

Your young correspondent probably won't have a clue on how to fold a piece of 8 ½" × 11" paper into thirds so that it will slide into an envelope. You'll want to have them practice that technique a few times. Do they know how to use an Elmer's glue stick to seal the envelope? Did you remind them that licking an envelope is not sanitary given the whole post-COVID-19 credo of "Don't blow out the candles on your birthday cake or get your saliva anywhere"? I've also turned a lot of kids onto using sealing wax and a wax stamp with their initials on it so they can drip hot red (or whatever color) wax onto the back of the envelope, then firmly press in their initials to secure the envelope flap. I've always loved doing that, and it's a pyromaniac's dream.

Opening the Envelope

Kids may not be familiar with how to *open* an envelope, either. I've gifted older kids their own letter openers (after they've been my pen pal for a while), and you'd think I gave them the biggest miracle in the world. Note: These are also known as paper knives, so make sure your child is old enough to handle a potential weapon! I just learned about battery-operated letter openers that make a clean slit.

Stationery

Paper-wise, I'm all over this category. You will need to provide prestamped and pre-addressed envelopes for a better chance of a response. Don't expect a blank card to be filled up by scintillating storytelling. Rather than despair about the lack of creativity, I created my own cards with multiple-choice questions when my grandson Sam was at camp and quite young. All Sam had to do was put a check mark next to the right answers. He turned those quizzes around quickly, and it was a kick to see his answers. As when I learned the details of my grandfather's daily life, it was exciting to hear what camper Sam was experiencing, eating, playing, and doing.

On the other hand, a regular card with embedded questions addressed to another grandchild at sleepaway camp flatlined completely. It didn't render a response. Even though I'd optimistically included a pen, I got nada. I admit, I was disappointed because I'd tried hard to connect. But after multiple attempts, even a gung-ho grandparent doesn't have the heart to keep being ghosted. At some point, it's okay to give up and acknowledge this is not the child's "love language."

When your teenage target audience member returns to civilization and has access to their desktop and printer, let them pound away on their beloved computer to compose the message and then print it. Teach them to personalize the look of a printed piece of paper—to underline a few words here or add exclamation marks there or draw a picture in the corner. (A good word to underline is always the sign-off, "Love.")

Office Depot and Staples carry inexpensive colored printer paper; cruise the school supplies aisle to find stickers or press-on foil stars to glitter things up. Look for cool Japanese stationery online. If you want a compact format that doesn't require a lot of sentences, postcards are the answer. The other benefit of a postcard is it fills up quickly!

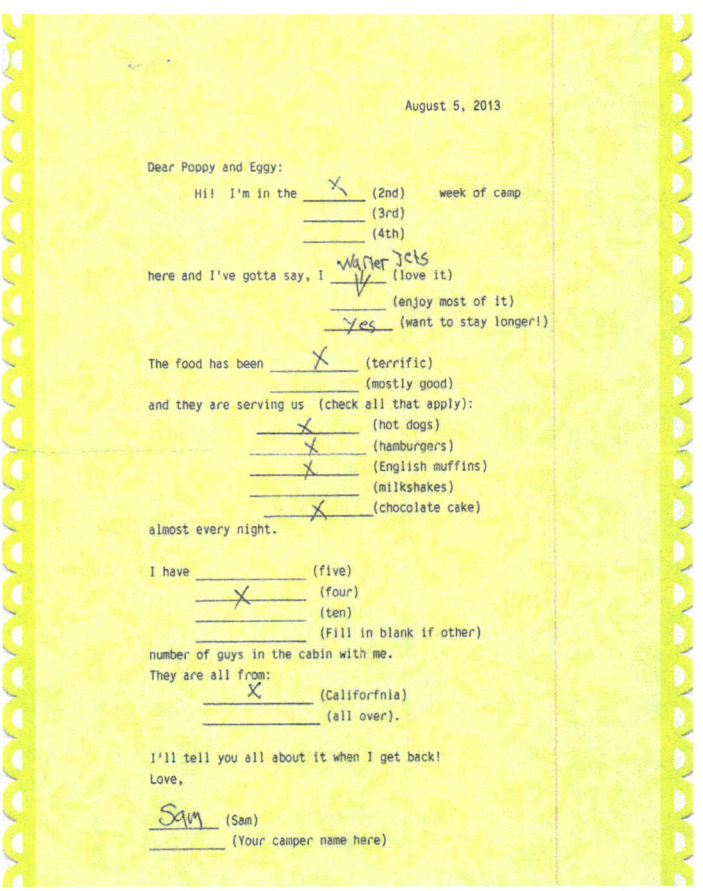

Checklist from Sam Swartz.

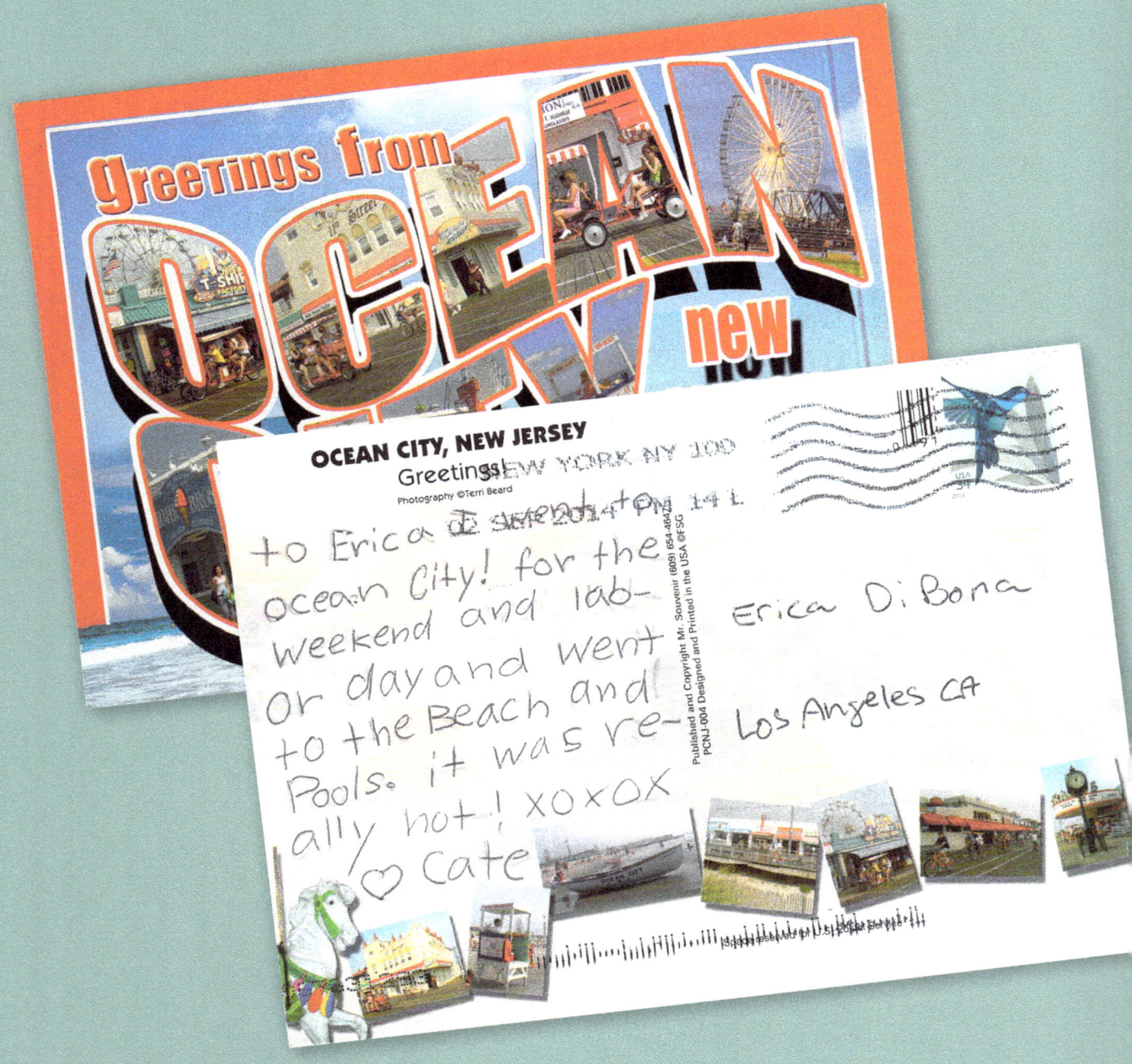

OCEAN CITY, NEW JERSEY
Greetings
Photography ©Terri Beard

to Erica I went to
ocean city! for the
weekend and lab-
or day and went
to the Beach and
pools. it was re-
ally hot! XOXOX
♡ Cate

Erica Di Bona

Los Angeles CA

Postcard from
Cate Ferrall.

My pen pal Cate, a college student from Brooklyn to whom I've been writing since she was four years old, was hooked because she couldn't wait to send a postcard from her trip to the Jersey Shore. Her dad told me that she was so excited she scribbled it in the car on the drive home.

How to Address an Envelope

If your young charges are not sure how to address an envelope, take a photo of this template with your phone and text it to them. I first spotted this in the mail room of Rhode Island School of Design for college kids to model. I thought that was horrifying, but evidently I needed to accept the reality that kids aren't familiar with sending letters.

When Short and Sweet Is Not Enough

Although it's always better to write something rather than nothing at all, some notes are hardly worth the postage they use. Not every note is a winner. Here's an example of one of those.

Vin and I have a favorite story about our friend's son Ian, who was thirteen and post-bar mitzvah. After the big event Ian dutifully disappeared into his bedroom and later emerged with sealed handfuls of Thank Yous. His parents, Lloyd and Sherry, were ecstatic.

Lloyd boasted, "Kid's working hard. We're blown away. He's almost done."

Vin congratulated him on raising a son with such excellent etiquette. Our Thank You note arrived a few days later: "Dear Erica and Vin, Thanks for the gift. Love, Ian."

"Oh shit." Vin wiped away tears of laughter. "Poor Lloyd has no idea."

Your name
Address Line 1
Address Line 2/Apartment Number (if necessary)
City, State, Zip code

Postage Stamp

Recipient (Who's getting it)
Address Line 1
Address Line 2 (if necessary)
City, State, Zip
Country (if not domestic)

Addressing a proper envelope.

"Maybe you should tell him before Ian sends more," I suggested.

The next day Vin took Lloyd aside, saying, "We received the note."

Lloyd beamed.

"Uh ... it's not quite what you think." Vin handed over Exhibit A.

Lloyd read it, his face flushing. "Son of a bitch! We wondered how he finished so many!"

When Version Two arrived, it was several sentences more specific. Lesson learned: Speedy turnaround is good, but details are better.

Creating a Happy Place to Write

To get your tykes to the table, make sure they have a welcoming, inspiring space to start their communication journey. This works for you too. Try to create a positive association with the act of sitting down to write. My childhood bedroom had a desk made from an upside-down door laid over two file cabinets, with my loden green Olympia typewriter perched on top. It was beyond basic, but I loved sitting in the brown leather secretary's chair, spinning around, and dreaming of one day being a boss in an office.

Have you shared your love of office supplies with your kids? Do they know how to seal an envelope with a glue stick, not their tongue? Or close it with washi tape or sealing wax? Do they have postage stamps and envelopes, and do they know what a mailbox is and how to put the envelope through the slot?

Don't be ashamed to use whatever tools you have to get your young correspondents inspired. It's okay to use bribes to incentivize. We all do better when there's a little sugar involved— sometimes literally! If they are older, promise to give them a gift card for whatever they're into. Be shameless—this is a tough game! Praise them when they *do* grind out a letter. Share how much it means to you and how much you eagerly

anticipate their next one. It's okay to guilt-trip them a bit when you *don't* hear from them. And similarly, compliment them when they *do* come through! If you're lucky, you may spark a bit of excitement in them, and the game is on.

Teach Them the Twin Values of Empathy and Diplomacy

Rest assured, by promoting letter writing, you're teaching the young people you influence two very important concepts that will span a lifetime: how to have empathy and how to practice diplomacy. As I shared with my daughter, if we could all add a little empathy for and understanding of each other, we could significantly lower the intensity of hostility between warring factions because each side has finally bothered to dig below the surface to find out what's important to the other—or to care about each other's differences.

A diplomatic letter may be the first overture to peace. Through practice, I have learned the tools of disarming people who may have ill will toward me or a difficult scenario. One of my most powerful tools for negotiating peace is writing my thoughts down with care and imagining how the other person might receive them—putting yourself in someone else's shoes and practicing sensitivity to their worldview. As a young person or even an old learner, using the "sandwich technique" is a great place to start, even with email correspondence.[21]

It's basically starting with a compliment, then saying what needs to be improved, and ending on another positive note. It sandwiches the bad news, if you will, between two nicer moments to make it more palatable.

Now that Part One has given you an understanding of the benefits and psychology of writing a thank you note—including the spreading of love and joy for your own health—we get to roll up our sleeves, sharpen our pencils, and uncover our typewriters for Part Two: Let's Get Writing! ●

Note from Rio
written on a
paper plane.

PART TWO

Let's Get Writing!

Chapter Six

How to Craft a Proper Thank You Letter

How fantastic would it feel to craft a note that changes a person's day or makes them want to keep it in their journal or showcase it in a frame on the wall? I am going to lead you through a system I've developed for writing a Thank You in three easy paragraphs called "Me, You, and Us."

If you follow these simple steps, people will reach out to proclaim you as the best Thank You writer ever! Also, the bar is super low because as I've mentioned before you are taking an action that 99 percent of the population is not doing! Don't be afraid. By doing this you're already a winner.

Three Parts of a Powerful Thank You Note: ME, YOU, and US

Me

1. Write About "Me"
Recall a Moment You Had with the Gift-Giver or Person Who Helped You

- Start the letter with "When I..." if you need a first sentence.
- Share how the experience made you feel— how it changed or touched your life.
- A "moment" is always a good way to frame the letter.
- Enhance the moment and tell them why you appreciate their gift or help.
- Think about your feelings <u>before you begin</u>. Genuinely time travel back to when they helped or gave you something and fully describe that overall experience (via the five senses) in your sentences.

First Sentence Examples:

- When we turned down the lights, the studio transformed.
- When they seated me next to you, I hit the jackpot ...
- The first thing we said when we woke up this morning was, "Wasn't that a perfect party at Norman Lear's last night?"
- From the moment we rang the bell, we sensed we were in for something different.

You

2. Write About "You" (The Other Person)
Tell the Receiver "Thanks for Being You"

- Say something nice about the person.
- Get them to fall a tiny bit in love with you. Make them feel special. Show them you appreciate them.
- Remind them how their talents affect the world.
- Talk about your relationship and how their kindness affects you.
- Thank *them* and share how you feel about them.
- Say, "I love what you did ... how you took the time to speak with me..."
- Reflect back on the positive qualities you see in the giver. This paragraph is *your* gift to them.
- Be honest so that the letter rings true.

Us

3. Write About "Us"
Bring It Back to Your Combined Future Together

- How could you enjoy the gift together in the future? For example, you were given a cookie-baking kit, so you suggest they come over and make cookies sometime.
- How can you keep the relationship going? What's the next step so that you become more involved? For example, you could save the bottle of wine they gave you to celebrate your friendship.

- Show where you're going next. For example, say you look forward to your next lunch or dinner—and that you're buying!
- Set the stage for your next encounter. For example, you may have discovered the recipient loves astronomy, so suggest going to the observatory together.
- Make a promise to stay in touch. Most people like to feel wanted and included; they are often looking to belong.
- Save the Thank You for the end.

You give away the punchline if you say the Thank You right at the top. The card will usually have "Thank You" printed on it or the recipient will guess it's a Thank You, so spend your precious real estate on deepening the relationship through your words.

Finally, proofread it before you send it out. Scan and save it for your files. You may want to craft a follow-up note later on, so it's helpful to know what you previously said.

Caveats: Don't let perfectionism hold you back. It's better to do something than nothing, even if it's just a couple sentences. Every letter doesn't have to be perfect.

Erica's Rules on Thank Yous

- Write back to the gift-giver while the emotion is fresh. The longer I wait, the more stale my memory gets and the more predictable my response becomes. Immediate immersion is like a twenty-minute sketch. If you're inspired, do it fast and get it done.
- Don't use the item until after you've written the note. (I won't eat the Godiva chocolates, wear the plum-colored silk scarf, or put ice cubes in the orchid plant until I've done this. It's my own time-keeper.) Incentivize yourself.
- Tell a colorful story. I always describe how I've used and enjoyed or reacted to the gift.

If the item is a bummer, placing the item in context will also divert the receiver's interest and make them think you're more enthusiastic than you actually are (see later guidance on "How to Wax Poetic About a Gift You Hate," starting on page 92).
- Employ the senses of touch, smell, sight, hearing, and taste where appropriate to enhance the description when you can.
- It *must* be legible. I say handwriting is not necessary—the letter can be written on a computer, printed out, and taped onto a card. If you have a typewriter, that's a bonus.
- Gather all your materials together for the thank you note project (I go into more detail in the chapter on tools).

> You give away the punchline if you say the Thank You right at the top. The card will usually have "Thank You" printed on it or the recipient will guess it's a thank you, so spend your precious real estate on deepening the relationship through your words.

THREE PARTS OF A
POWERFUL "THANK YOU" NOTE *

ME

1. WRITE ABOUT "ME"
Go back to the MOMENT YOU HAD THE EXPERIENCE.

Start it with "When I..." if you need a first sentence.
- [ ] Share how it made you feel – how it changed or touched your life.
- [ ] A "moment" is always a good way to frame it.
- [ ] Describe that epiphany to make the Donor feel they're back there with you.
- [ ] Enhance the moment & tell them why you appreciate their help.
- [ ] Think about your feelings before you begin. Genuinely 'time-transport' back and reflect that in your sentences.

YOU

2. WRITE ABOUT "YOU" (THE OTHER PERSON)
"THANK YOU FOR BEING YOU".

Find nice things to say about the person.
- [ ] Get them to fall a tiny bit in love with you. Make them feel special.
- [ ] Show them you appreciate them.
- [ ] Remind them how their talents affect the world.
- [ ] Talk about how you see your relationship with them, and how their kindness affects you directly.
- [ ] Thank THEM and share how you feel about them.

US

3. WRITE ABOUT "US"
BRING IT BACK TO YOUR COMBINED FUTURE TOGETHER.

How can we work together someday?
- [ ] What can I do going forward to help keep the person close to what's going on with me? What's the next step so they become more involved?
- [ ] Make a promise of together-ness. Most people like to feel wanted & included. They, too, are often looking to belong.

And finally: Proofread it before you send it out. Scan/save it for your files. You may want to send another and it's helpful to know what you said before, as well as useful to build your files.

*From a presentation by Erica Gerard Di Bona

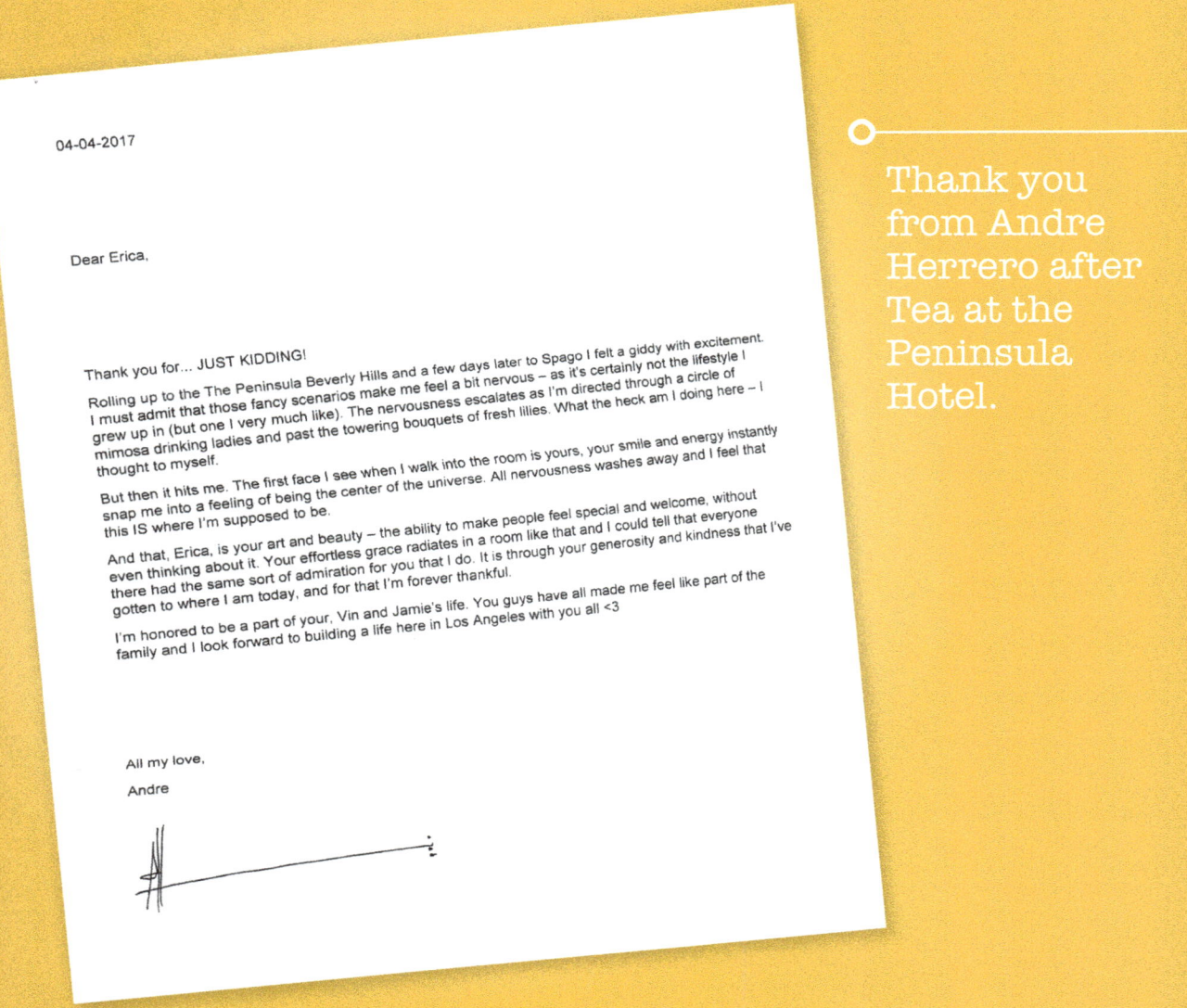

04-04-2017

Dear Erica,

Thank you for... JUST KIDDING!

Rolling up to the The Peninsula Beverly Hills and a few days later to Spago I felt a giddy with excitement. I must admit that those fancy scenarios make me feel a bit nervous – as it's certainly not the lifestyle I grew up in (but one I very much like). The nervousness escalates as I'm directed through a circle of mimosa drinking ladies and past the towering bouquets of fresh lilies. What the heck am I doing here – I thought to myself.

But then it hits me. The first face I see when I walk into the room is yours, your smile and energy instantly snap me into a feeling of being the center of the universe. All nervousness washes away and I feel that this IS where I'm supposed to be.

And that, Erica, is your art and beauty – the ability to make people feel special and welcome, without even thinking about it. Your effortless grace radiates in a room like that and I could tell that everyone there had the same sort of admiration for you that I do. It is through your generosity and kindness that I've gotten to where I am today, and for that I'm forever thankful.

I'm honored to be a part of your, Vin and Jamie's life. You guys have all made me feel like part of the family and I look forward to building a life here in Los Angeles with you all <3

All my love,
Andre

Thank you from Andre Herrero after Tea at the Peninsula Hotel.

- Don't say Thank You until the end. Tease them! Why blow the lead? They'll have to keep reading.

Jamie's college friend Andre Herrero once wrote me after he attended an etiquette class I gave to Rhode Island School of Design alumni. I'd emphasized, "Save the thank you for the end," so when I reviewed Andre's post-class product I thought, "So much for *that* lesson!" Psych. He nailed it.

Using the Five Senses to Describe a Gift

I call this practice "letting yourself marinate in the gift" before you write a word to evoke a sensorial experience that leads to a more personalized Thank You. Don't write a note in a rush and don't let too much time go by—the longer you delay, the more difficult it will be to remember and summon the emotions

Erica Gerard Di Bona

April 19, 2017

Mr. Andre Herrero

Dear Andre:

I loved your "psych" start --
"Thank you for ... JUST KIDDING!"

That said to me right away that you 'got it' -- and the rest of your letter was so fascinating, thoughtful and feel-good that I felt the pride of a college professor who sees their student achieve greater heights than either of them ever thought possible.

You now have more tools in your quiver, besides the special rub-out compound you used on Jamie's car (and thank you for that!) -- and these correspondence tips already seem to be incorporated readily and easily into your writing ...

I love the things you said about me, too, in the "All about You" part. The funny thing is, you made them seem like they were true ... and that, my friend, is the mark of a great "Thank You".

Love,

Erica Gerard Di Bona
Erica Gerard Di Bona

Check out my blog: ArtofThankYou.com

Thank you letter from Erica to Andre Herrero post-Tea.

---

that bubbled over when you first saw the gift. It's almost like you need to reach a meditative state to vibe with the gift again and the person who gave it to you. Time travel back to when you first opened it: Hear the ripping of the wrapping paper and see if you can describe that deliriously happy and eternally grateful reaction. And if you're weren't deliriously happy? Stay tuned for a helpful talk about subtext.

Keep the gift near where you are writing the letter. Spend a few minutes admiring it from all angles, thinking about what prompted the gift-giver to find it for you and fantasizing about how you intend to use it going forward. I hope you have not already eaten it, worn it, or tucked it away in a drawer somewhere. It becomes increasingly difficult to write exuberantly about a half-gnawed box of chocolate, droopy or dead flowers, or a dirty sweater (since you ignored my suggestion and donned it *before* you did your homework).

1. **Sight:** What does it look like? How does the light fall on it? How does it blend in with your décor? How similar is it to something you've been wanting but didn't purchase for yourself?

2. **Sound:** Does it make a noise? What does it remind you of when you hear it? Does it take you back to another time or to a childhood memory? What does it trigger when you hear it? Does it calm you down? Does it get you energized and ready to take a road trip or remind you of riding your bike when you were a kid? Does it evoke the whoosh of the ocean or the wind in the trees? Does it remind you of the patter of raindrops, a calming sound that reminds you of evenings inside when you crawl under a blanket and write in your journal?

3. **Taste:** Describe how it affects your tongue. Is it salty, bitter, sour, or sweet? Does it remind you of another favorite food? Does it take you back to your childhood and a happy memory?

4. **Smell:** Does its fragrance dot the air around it? Does it smell like your signature scent? Does it remind you of being outside after a summer rainstorm? What does the scent remind you of (in a positive way)?

5. **Touch:** Does it have a certain pressure or vibration that hits the receptors in your body? Does it relieve tension or help massage your poor back?

> "Short and sweet" can be just as wonderful as an extensive epistle. The bottom line is, you want the reader to feel better after ingesting your compliments. A Thank You is a Thank You no matter what medium.

Unorthodox Thank Yous

I've spent most of this book exhorting you to inscribe full-on letters to thank someone. I want to clarify that a Thank You doesn't have to be in an orthodox form. Sometimes it's just as wonderful to receive a few words on a hotel room notepad or a lined index card tucked into the front of a book.

I stopped working in TV production when I became a new mother at age thirty-four. For the first time in my life, I began watching morning shows. My favorite was a new offering called *The View*, where witty politicos and sassy comediennes debated politics, sex, and "hot topics."

One day the on-air ladies were comparing "road warrior" stories when comedienne Joy Behar dropped a bombshell: "Do you realize when you leave a tip for the hotel maid at the end of your stay, you're not giving it to the staff equally? The person who services the room the day you check out gets the money. You should leave a little each morning."

Thank you note from maid.

My dormant inner socialist came alive. I'd assumed everyone shared. I vowed to leave five bucks *each morning*.

I tried this on a trip to Providence, Rhode Island (I'm a former trustee for the Rhode Island School of Design). The Renaissance Marriott is my home away from home. Everyone's friendly, and they accommodate my OCD travel requests. (No noisy elevator nearby, no blocked view, no fingerprints on furniture, and extra notepads and towels daily.)

On my first morning, I scrawled a message on a personalized buck slip I'd brought from home and placed $5 on it. (I bring my own notepads when I travel since paper is not always in the room.) I'd do this to say, "Thank You, Housekeeping."

When I returned that evening, I looked to see if the mouse ate the cheese. My offering was gone, and the cleaning lady had left *me* something on a Post-it: "Thank you very much." Under her words she'd drawn a happy face.

I left another note and tip the next morning.

She responded: "Thank you very much. I am happy."

When I travel, a phantom makes the bed and exchanges post-shower towels for fluffy clean white ones. It's a disembodying feeling to have a hardworking stranger sanitize your surroundings. My personal note creates the chance to appreciate someone invisible. A smiley face from the maid is a low-tech emoji for "thank you." Maybe it's my imagination, but when I leave a message—and sometimes get one in return—it somehow makes the room feel more like home.

Whatever the format or length of the note, warmth and genuine kindness fill the space. Paper size and word length aren't as important as the feelings you convey.

"Short and sweet" can be just as wonderful as an extensive epistle. The bottom line is, you want the reader to feel better after ingesting your compliments. A Thank You is a Thank You no matter what medium.

Tools for the Thank You

We saw how a Thank You can be a very simple, appreciative one-line note if it's as genuine as what the housekeeper wrote. But scribing notes for gifts is painful for most of us. Although you may agree it's important to respond to a gift, every part of you screams, "*How?*"

You're not prepared. You don't own stationery (though hopefully you know what it is). Where's a pen that works or the nearest official blue USPS mailbox? How much does a Forever° stamp cost? (Answer: As of July 13, 2025, it is seventy-eight cents for a one-ounce letter. Each additional ounce is twenty-nine cents.) Where can you buy postage without entering a U.S. Post Office? How long is "Forever"?

Once you acquire basic tools, there are other impediments. If your excuse is "My handwriting has gone to shit," I get it. My scrawl is so squished and ugly that I can't decode my own notes. This is where I break with Emily Post, the esteemed etiquette expert. I say—*brace yourself, purists*—it's okay to type your message. Have you ever received correspondence where the handwriting was so garbled you had to squint to decipher it? Overly florid cursive is dramatic but impractical and difficult to read. Teeny-tiny printing isn't any better.

Retire your pen or pencil if your handwriting is unreadable. Use the printer after you've composed the prose on your computer. If it's one that allows you to print out in color, that's a bonus. Pull out a typewriter (if you have one) or retrieve the Smith Corona portable in its tan carrying case tucked away in your grandmother's closet.

If you express yourself through images and you're a better photographer than writer, take a picture of a gift after you've received it and text it to the giver. When I used to order flowers or takeout meals for my mom and my nephew Ian, her caretaker, Ian was Johnny-on-the-spot about including me in the moment. He prepared the dinner and shot it so that I could virtually join them at the table as they dug into their well-presented plates. I would wander past the front hall entry on my FaceTime view from my nephew's phone and see where he'd placed the pink lilies in their new clear vase. My mother, who lived to ninety-six, used to write Thank You notes, but it became difficult near the end. When Ian was looking out for her as her condition worsened, I didn't expect either of them to send a snail mail Thank You, so the pictures and texts more than satisfied my need to know my food or flowers had arrived safely and were appreciated.

Not many of us reach for a pen and paper, and I'm cool with that.

Go ahead, feel free to use your computer. Try to be creative. There are some easy ways to make your generated material look unique. People *do* pay attention to font—avoid Papyrus or Comic Sans unless you *really* love it. If your calligraphy is as elegant as the day you learned it, carry on, and congratulations. A few older ladies I correspond with land their sentences on invisible lines straight as railroad tracks. They're the exception, I'm afraid. Today, cursive is taught for less than a full year in elementary schools. I'll bet that within the decade, handwriting will disappear altogether. When was the last time you generated something in longhand? I'll wager you don't scribble checks, blue Bic ballpoint in hand—you do it electronically.

So now you're seated at your beloved computer, ready to go. But wait a second— what will you print the letter on? That brings us to my favorite topic (besides typewriters): paper products.

Creating Your Own Design

If you want a polished image and better branding and have extra time and money, design your own letterhead. A website like VistaPrint lets you create personalized cards or stationery. If you prefer your message short and sweet, choose a 5" × 7" size—less space to fill. (The problem with 8 ½" × 11" size paper is you need more than a few lines to make your final product look like something.) Include your snail mail address if you want to receive a response that way. Add your phone number(s), email address, website(s), and social media site handles.

If you love selfies, create an original Thank You card that's an homage to you. Upload a picture of yourself, something that relates to your business, hobbies, or favorite animal, or whatever else makes you happy. Play with your design. It's only paper, and if you hate what you did, you can always produce a second batch. If you're in love, design a "twofer" featuring you and your life partner. It's handy when you're responding to the folks who gave you wedding gifts, and having your home address preprinted (as you did on your stationery) saves you a step.

Embossed foil for the envelope doubles the price, so don't go for that right away, if at all. Notecards on VistaPrint.com start at $9.99 for ten cards with envelopes. And VistaPrint isn't the only option. For example, Collage.com also produces photo blankets, photo pillows, and tote bags if you're really trying to make an impression!

If you're one of the few people who uses a typewriter, like me, commit the letter to a piece of paper, cut it to size, and paste it inside the card. Or try this trick: Type it directly onto a white shipping label (e.g., choose the Avery True Block label, #8465). I estimate how much space I have to fill on the birthday / anniversary / whatever-it-is card. I put a larger piece of

two-sided paper in my typewriter and write out the message. Then I cut my words to fit the note where I want to position it, peel off the backing, and voilà! People marvel at how I do it; it's painless and gets big results.

Items You'll Need to Craft Thank You Stamps

First, where can you buy stamps? You can visit your nearest United States Postal Service office in person. If that gives you the heebie-jeebies, avoid the line and buy them online through the USPS website (USPS.com), called, appropriately enough, "Stamps & Supplies." There's also a drop-down menu that creates prepaid labels for flat-rate packages or other box sizes you typically need (see "Click-N-Ship"). You can even purchase sustainable products that use 98 percent recycled content at Costco.com. These stamps

> If you want a polished image and better branding and have extra time and money, design your own letterhead.

usually feature the U.S. flag, but online, you can find flower patterns too.

There's also an expensive way to beat everyone else: If you have an extra $31.40 to spend, copy what my friend Helen Hintz does when she "absolutely, positively" wants to get a letter there overnight. She'll send hers by Priority Mail Express through USPS. This method is expensive, but if you don't trust your postal service to deliver your piece in a day, it's a backup option you should know about. When I was handed the white 8 ½" × 11" hard cardboard envelope from her, it was a thrill. What was so important it merited $31.40 to send? I felt valued, honored, and humbled. Inside was a four-page letter Helen had written in response to one of mine. (When I called to let her know the express mail arrived, I advised her that she could have saved money by using the flat-rate option for around $8. She politely reminded me that flat rate is *not* guaranteed for one-day arrival. The Hintz family had been experiencing severe mail service breakdowns in New Jersey. My friend didn't want hers to somehow get "lost" in the system. Point taken.)

Amazon, the perennial online marketplace, carries Forever® stamps, too, and also sells the additional one-ounce twenty-nine-cent (as of July 13, 2025) stamp. Their prices seem to vary, and vendors aren't scrupulous about selling them at actual market value.

Get the self-adhesive kind, not the ones on a roll (they call it a "coil") unless you like licking each one as you put it on the envelope!

Check how recent the stamp image is. Does it look homemade? I'd caution not to buy from a third-party vendor in case the stamps aren't the real deal. Unfortunately, stamp counterfeiting has been around since the first postage stamp, the "Penny Black," was issued in Great Britain in 1840. The "Penny Black" was the first stamp to be introduced and within the next year, people had mailed more than seventy million letters! Three years later, more than 210 million letters were sent.

There's no such thing as discount postage. You should pay seventy-three cents for each first-class stamp in a book of one hundred stamps ($78) and no more. No less than face value is a tip-off that it's not the real thing.

Scammers are out there making fake stamps, which they peddle on social media marketplaces, e-commerce sites (where they use third-party vendors), and other websites. During Christmas 2023, this became a huge problem and made the nightly news because millions of counterfeit stamps were being offered by online sellers. Be wary of or totally avoid sponsored ads. Real stamps made by the U.S. government use special paper and added watermarks for security.

I'm weird. I don't mind standing in line at the post office, but I'm in the minority. It's fun to people-watch and kill time to break up my desk-bound day. Don't go at rush hour on a Friday. (The customers are tired, crabby, and

> Decorate the envelope to showcase your personality— feature a hobby, dream, or historic figure you admire.

How to Craft a Proper Thank You Letter — Erica Gerard Di Bona

tense, and the staff feels the same. No wonder USPS workers "go postal" from answering stupid questions from over-caffeinated customers who procrastinated on shipping their boxes and don't want to pay express rates.)

The benefit of going in person to my local postal station is I can study their display of new stamps. If you don't want to disappear into the mind-blowing world of stamps with me, skip the rest of this paragraph! With stamps, there are ever-changing offerings, from "Fruits & Vegetables" to "American Gardens" to commemorative versions. The "Total Eclipse of the Sun" stamp honored the 2017 total solar eclipse, featuring a first-ever design in thermochromic ink that reacted to your body heat when you touched it. "Stamp Out Breast Cancer" and "Save Vanishing Species" stamps cost a few dollars more and benefit that cause. There are round stamps like "Global: Chrysanthemum" to send overseas ($1.65 apiece). You can even find stamps featuring frogs, coral reefs, Meyer lemons, astronauts, Henry James, hip-hop artists, Halloween silhouettes, Bugs Bunny, dinosaurs, winter scenes, silver coffeepots, and imagery from holidays like Kwanzaa, Christmas, and Hanukkah. "Thank you" stamps come in sage green, navy, maroon, and aqua.

You can go crazy with options. Decorate the envelope to showcase your personality—feature a hobby, dream, or historic figure you admire. That top right-hand corner of the envelope is another opportunity to show off who you are and give your receiver a hint before they delve into the letter itself. I don't suggest you use the standard American flag stamp for friends and people you want to impress with your new Thank You skills. Save those for bills!

Letter Opener

Another item you might consider adding to your desk is a letter opener. They are made of

Erica with her favorite Kate Spade purse.

My dad always said, "Life is about keeping yourself entertained."

wood and metal (stainless steel, silver, or pewter), ivory, or plastic and might have an embellished handle. Some have a retractable razor blade inside a plastic handle, but I've never touched one because there's a hundred percent guarantee I'd cut myself! Oh, and don't run with knives, it's never a good idea.

Envelope Surprises

Remember how excited you were when you opened your first fortune cookie? It's fun to be flabbergasted. If I'm doing a business outreach, I'll add my business card. It's amusing to tuck in flat embellishments when appropriate, such as:

- Bookmarks (if your organization publishes them, even better).
- Gift certificates and gift cards (if the recipient has a secure mailbox).
- Lottery tickets (same as above).
- Pop-open cards with messages inside. I like a brand called Compendium, with messages ranging from "Smile" to "Yay You" to "Thank You." They are easy to purchase online or at some stationery stores. I've found them at general merchandise stores, too, in the party and office supplies section.

My dad always said, "Life is about keeping yourself entertained." If you enjoy the artistry of the envelope you've created, it's likely your recipient will too.

I beg you and promise to hold your hand—try to overcome your fear of snail mail. As the Nike ad campaign urges, "Just do it." Post it (in the mail, not online) and see what happens! An envelope generally takes a day or two to arrive at its destination, or up to five days if you're sending it back east. The results will convince you. It's the difference between the taste of homemade lasagna over frozen. The slower-paced way is more unique. You can feel the love in it, and it's totally worth the effort.

How to Wax Poetic About a Gift You Hate

Some presents are clunkers. The last-minute pasta machine for your girlfriend who, you remember as you wrap it, is gluten-free. Christmas Eve cufflinks for the hoody-wearing techie. A bottle of Scotch for the recovered alcoholic. Lilacs for the travel agent who's violently allergic to flowers. Hail Mary passes. The "Oh well" factor or "I bought it at Nordstrom, they can exchange it."

There are a million and one scenarios for a gift gone wrong. Imagine this: You and your fiancée are sitting cross-legged on your uncomfortable "Sofa for Less," staring at an ornate iron sunflower doorstop—yours because you gallantly and stupidly opted *not* to have your wedding registry at Crate & Barrel. What do you say?

If you don't adore a gift, find a way to say anything as a decoy that implies you loved *something* about it but doesn't specifically mention *what*. For example: "The Italian cookbook reminded me of all the eggplant caponata and freshly caught swordfish we ate on our trip to Sicily and inspires me to get back in the kitchen. My husband will thank you for that too!" (Subtext: I may go in the kitchen, but it doesn't mean I'm going to whip up anything from this cookbook or any other.)

First, place the gift in front of you. Try to pick up its vibes and welcome it into your emotional world. You want to experience a positive feeling so that you can write about it, even if it doesn't ring your bell. Anything that comes into your house is sacred.

Remember, I don't use, eat, or wear a gift until after I've produced a note. I don't put it away, either, because if I stick it in a drawer or hide it in a closet, it'll be "out of sight, out of mind"—which means I'll never write that message of gratitude.

Not feeling inspired? Marinate in it a bit. Study it, see how it's constructed, notice its smell. Un-filter your literal, truthful brain and find something nice to say. Look for a starting point. I begin with how it will make my life complete. Remember the concept of diplomacy through subtext? How to say one thing and mean another? Consider this your lesson on Subtext 101.

Examples:

You write: "The flowers will brighten the room."
Subtext: "They'll brighten the room while I sneeze my head off because I'm allergic to them."

You write: "The iron daisy will control our naughty front door that refuses to stay shut."
Subtext: "I hope a strong wind knocks it over and breaks it."

You write: "The Macallan Scotch will give our friends a warm welcome on a wintry night."
Subtext: "I'll never drink it, so I hope I can find friends who will."

See how diplomacy works? Don't declare *you'll* use it; rather, indicate *it will find a use*. Imply you'll care about it, even if you re-gift it to an unsuspecting friend.

S-t-r-e-t-c-h the truth, baby, like when you pretended size didn't matter with Boyfriend #2.

Here are some more things you can write and what they really mean:

"I've always wanted one!"
What it means: But never so much I actually *bought* one.

"I've dreamed of this for years."
Translation: In my nightmares.

Dear Chuck & Ava:
December 13, 2013
One pear (from the bottom box, largest in the stack) is already devoured. I looked at it last night -- around midnight-- and determined I'd break into the foil this morning. I took one bite and it was as wickedly evil as Eve must have felt, biting into the red apple in the Garden of Eden. Jamie and I unwrapped the other fruitful boxes (all of which are worth re-using). Baklava. Chocolate almonds. Popcorn w/chocolate. Salmon! A bounty of items, every single one worthy of the calories. We will enjoy them from top to bottom, and we thank you for getting us the fanciest display item Harry & David features. I've always wanted to see their top-shelf present -- and now, thanks to you, we've got one in our kitchen! A wonderful bounty, and we thank you for this & everything.
Love,
Erica &
Vin

Thank You to my dear friends Chuck and Ava, who have since passed on, for a very thoughtful gift.

Erica Di Bona

June 30, 2012

Dear Lori,

Where do I begin? With the orange scarf, which I've already worn several times and combined with everything from green to orange to cream? That screams "Summer" and "fun", "glittery" and "elegant", simultaneously while it whispers "elegance"?

I have a bright orange Polo silk shirt that I shlepped all the way to Switzerland, RISD, Harvard and home, and never wore once...because it was just a little too...BRIGHT... and as I sat here admiring your scarf, I thought, "Aha! That could be the way to tone down the bright orange shirt, keep it all Ralph Lauren, and make it more fun at the same time." So you've coordinated an outfit for me without even knowing it...another attribute to your extreme ability to shop for those you love.

Speaking of shopping: again, I don't know where to begin. In TV lingo, you've "stumped the band". Usually, I can look at a gift and describe it. I tell the person who gave it to me how I'll use it, and after a few lauditory sentences, I've covered the bases.

With this travel kit by "Lori O", I honestly don't have the words to explain how overwhelmed I am by your attention to include EVERYTHING you love and travel with, and to "teach me the ways", just as you did on my wedding night to Josh, when you trotted me around the mall to find Frederick's of Hollywood, when you exhorted me to try something 'different', and when with your urging, I went from 'white' to 'black'.

page two, continued...

I look through the cunning display of tiny, individual sized samples. At the Vera Bradley blue paisley bag, how you've stuffed it full of everything you love, to share with me, to show me the way once again, as you did that wedding night...as you have encouraged me with Jamie, as you have helped me push it out with different clothes, jeans, even studded shoes!

Lint removing sheets. Wrinkle away, no steamer required. Didn't even know they carried that. Still using your 'foot/heel guard' you turned me onto before... Magnifying mirror, yes yes yes, in pink, even more exciting than I've found anywhere on my own. Cup -- great idea. No more cooties. Teeth items, exciting and what I'd take anyway, but now they're all in their own little place, condensed, minding their manners, instead of my way thrown into a large Ziplock bag full of air & banging around. Just tried the Body Butter. Yum. Didn't notice that before. Looking at it all. Taking it all in. How much time, effort, thought you went to. How much love you poured into this gift. What a loving person you are. Eye cream containers cuter than anything I've spotted. You're better than Oprah. Oprah could learn from YOU. And tomorrow I'll begin to pack, trying to condense, conserve, do it the "Lori way". You are truly a great friend, a dear person, and someone I know will always be two steps ahead of me, but open-hearted to help me catch up. Thank you for all you do for me...always.

Love, Erica

○───────────────────────────

Thank You to
Lori Otelsberg.

"It adds a certain élan to the room."
You're trying to say: Ugly, ugly, ugly.

"How did you know (insert name of color here) was my favorite color?"
You play coy: It's obvious you didn't.

It's fun to convince yourself a horrible gift is nice. Remember, the giver's intent was pure when they purchased it. Whether the red horizontal stripes on the bright orange leggings make you look grotesque, the grapefruit candle smells rancid, or the chartreuse lingerie makes your untanned legs look sickly, your friend or relative spent time and resources to shop, wrap, and ship the gift. (Unless they bought it online—but it still wasn't free.) Lavish consideration on your Thank You note, just as they thought of you while they chose your gift. I've found that as I reexamine what they sent me, I come to appreciate it even more. Describe your positive feelings and share the moment with them. You'll feel better, and who knows? You may grow to love that iron daisy doorstop—or not.

Scorching Thank Yous

When my first husband, Josh, and I got married, we were on a shoestring budget, so when my ex-boyfriend Jeff offered to shoot our wedding for free, we were thrilled. As News Director at a local television station, Jeff had access to camera crews. On the big day, the cameraman and audio man captured the "I do" and interviewed guests making funny comments. We were dancing and eating and drinking—until all of a sudden, the guys ran up, out of breath. There was a four-alarm fire close by, fueled by gasoline under the street, and the Assignment Manager needed all hands on deck. Whoever arrives on scene earliest owns the story, and Jeff's crew was right around

the corner. It's all about audience share and the highest ratings. The live truck and team left, and our party raged on.

Weeks later, our wedding tapes arrived. Excited, we watched our ceremony, all as we remembered it. We inserted the next videotape, "Party," but saw chaos as firefighters aimed hoses at leaping flames amid red and gray clouds of smoke.

"What the f***?" I didn't know whether to laugh or cry—or both. I called Jeff the next day, and he explained: The live truck crew ran out of videotape cassettes, and the only ones on hand were—you guessed it—mine. They obliterated our big day to commemorate the bigger story (in their minds, at least).

When I sat down to compose my Thank You, I was still pissed. I scrawled part of my message on the card's top fold. Then I took a match and burned the edges underneath until it was only partially legible *and* smudged with carbon. My line: "Not every wedding can compete with a four-alarm fire."

As an aside, the Fairfax District fire was no laughing matter. Twenty-three people were hurt when a mysterious gas explosion from a long-abandoned oil field shattered the walls and windows of a Ross Dress for Less. The

Lavish consideration on your Thank You note, just as they thought of you while they chose your gift.

blast was felt three blocks away. Fires spread throughout the night, and cars and stores were severely damaged.

There can also be hidden humorous messages in your not-so-veiled threats. My friend Kate Brinegar-Cowan and I fell into a "let's top each other" competition when I learned she celebrates St. Patrick's Day—with gusto. I began sending her garish emerald green deely boppers, knee-high shamrock socks, beer mugs, house flags, and more. Kate was a good sport and claimed she actually used a few of the items. But after a while, she wrote: "Two can play this game!"

She corralled horrible, tacky Hanukkah memorabilia, her latest offering being an aqua sweatshirt with mustard yellow menorahs and Stars of David and a bespectacled man's head saying, "Have a Pretty Pretty Pretty good Hanukkah." Now our messages say, "Wait," or "I'll get you." We look forward to outdoing each other, and it's added high-spirited play to the holidays for both of us.

Box decorated with discarded typewriter keys — gifted to Erica by Darlene Basch.

How To Be Gracious When It's Hideous

My father used to say, "Life is about keeping yourself entertained." In a way, writing a note of gratitude bundled around a bit of attitude makes me happy. I can entertain myself with my response, and I don't have to be saccharine sweet. I can allude to the shortcomings of a gift if I'm careful not to offend the giver. True graciousness is figuring how to thank someone in a genuine way while still being true to your own values. Not every gift hits the bullseye. Not every offering is just what you wanted. As long as you can find *some* positive aspect of it and highlight that in a meaningful way, you'll convince the gift-giver they made you happy—which they did, really, because isn't it the thought that counts?

Thank Yous are a way to capture life's moments, whether by poking fun at how a camera crew bungled shooting your wedding or enjoying a friend's gentle teasing about your holiday. A letter is a form of motion capture, a time stamp of how you're feeling that day.

Not every letter has to be brilliant. Don't punish yourself if you don't feel particularly inspired when you send out a note. A one-sentence postcard is still wonderful if you are being genuine and writing it from your heart. Don't agonize over making it the longest essay known to man. In short, have fun with your output.

You're not sending the note to nab a job (we'll cover that next) or to be glued into the family scrapbook. It's to commemorate a gift someone gave you, your appreciation for it, and the gracious continuation of the relationship you two share. With any luck, your correspondence will deepen the friendship and persuade the other person to be your pal for *years* to come.

A Thank You is a secret language between you and your recipient—a holy moment between two people. ●

Typewriter Paper

Once upon a ~~time~~ typewriter...

MADE IN ANALOG
APPRECIATION FOR
DESKTOP DISPLAY

ALL YOUR NOTE-
TAKING NEEDS.

1 ROLL OF
PERFORATED
NOTEPAPER SHEETS

54 SHEETS

ROOM TO STASH
SUPPLIES

A fun typewriter desktop display featuring perforated typewriter notepaper sheets.

Chapter Seven

Thank You Letters for Your Job Search

You've had the interview in person or over Zoom and feel pretty good about your chances. You were concise, laying out the responsibilities you've had, how you've managed conflicts or problems, and ultimately how your actions beat deadlines and saved your employer money. Now it's time to put the icing on the cake with the "post-interview thank you" adding an additional level of prominence to your presentation.

With your knowledge of the fundamentals of writing a Thank You, you have clever composition skills to add to your toolbox for landing your dream job. With a post-interview Thank You, you can break through the noise, blow away the competition, and stand out as you seek to land the job of your dreams. Since email is faster and you want to access the boss or human resources folks immediately, first send the Thank You electronically—but I hope you won't stop there. Button it up with a snail mail letter and you may tilt the odds in your favor.

A Thank You note is your last chance to sell yourself, a non-stealth excuse to rejigger another point of contact. As the CEOs of major companies receive 70 emails a day and the average person receives 121 emails a day, sending snail mail makes you unique. A top-level executive often compresses their response times to twice daily: They read and generate emails in the morning and at the end of the work day (or like my husband, it's the last thing he accomplishes before he walks away from the desktop and then again before he goes into work).

With texts, tweets, Instagram posts, TikToks, Facebook updates, and so on, we are all saturated with computer-generated messages. Although I advocate the instant action of sending an email after an interview, the saturation of communication the receiving party likely experiences proves "a letter is better." A beautiful way to easily send a snail mail thank you after an interview is to use the "scan and send snail mail double-hit."

1. Scan the nice paper letter you wrote (or typed, if your handwriting is awful).
2. Drop a full-size scan of your letter into the body of an email (most people won't open attachments). You don't need to write a detailed paragraph letting them know there is a scan there. The subject line should simply say, "Thank You Letter for Interview."
3. Then put that *actual* nice paper version into an envelope and trust the USPS to deliver it. The derisive term "snail mail" has crept into our vocabulary because some people doubt the postal service's speed. But in this case, you don't have to worry about how long it will take because you've covered yourself by sending the scan by email. By the time your recipient gets the envelope in the mail, they will have already seen your email outreach, and the real version will be the vanilla icing on the chocolate cake.
4. The scanned letter should be full-size so it's not a strain to read. You can repeat exactly what you wrote in your snail mail version at the top of your email so that the recipient will see it twice—once in the email and then again when they open their real mail a few days later.

A Thank You note is your last chance to sell yourself, a non-stealth excuse to rejigger another point of contact.

do i look like i give a rat's ass?

The point is, they will receive the scanned letter by email, possibly forget to reply, and then be reminded of that email by the snail mail! **It's a double play to get in front of the person twice.**

The Post-Interview Thank You

There is speculation by some, including the "woke patrol," that sending a letter to someone who helped or interviewed you is in itself an act of elitism. The theory goes that first-generation students or kids from a lower socioeconomic background were not necessarily taught how to value or produce post-event correspondence. In the U.S., such students or those from marginalized communities are already disadvantaged in some marketplaces, like the corporate world, by not knowing "soft skills" (i.e., the ability to communicate with prospective clients, problem-solving, work ethic, critical thinking, and conflict management). Not all households teach children how to interact, what to wear, and how to follow up in a professional context. Still, this shouldn't dissuade you from putting your best foot forward. If you don't do it, someone else will.

A top video game company executive once declared he had absolutely no time for post-interview Thank Yous in that company's impersonal, tech-oriented culture. He explained that if the interviews are outsourced, he may not meet candidates until the last hiring round. I wondered how prevalent this "don't bother" attitude was, and I worried that maybe my entire premise of "Thank Yous are important" was no longer relevant.

I queried Michael Seales, a UC Santa Cruz alum who counsels students at his alma mater, all of whom are eager to break into the video game industry. He is involved in the tech world as a software engineer at Riot Games, an American video game developer, publisher, and esports tournament organizer. *League of Legends* is the first free-to-play game the company launched. Michael designs apps, services, and distributed

Most importantly, the letter must feel authentic.

systems. He confirmed that in his world, a letter can work *against* a candidate if it feels like it came out of a book or the person is doing it for the sake of etiquette.

He said, "It doesn't move my needle," and if it's "unexpected or unusual, [it] could be interpreted as the wrong intent." If it came after an "informational interview," he felt it was more appropriate. He added, "If it says, 'Thanks, I appreciated your time and I learned something about how to work in this field,' it can have either a neutral or positive impact."

Most importantly, the letter must feel *authentic*. Michael reminded me that the world is becoming paperless and that an email is already "more formal" than a text and may be considered sufficient. New forms of communication are being created, too. Younger students, in school clubs, gaming groups, the art community, or just through friends, are migrating to apps like Discord to talk or hang out every day as they livestream games. He explained that many companies outsource recruiting because hiring the right staff is so expensive. Many companies conduct two or three interviews with a candidate until the recruiter, future employer, or placement agency makes the correct decision. Sometimes the candidate will be called back again if there is another excellent candidate going for the same job and the company needs to decide between them. It costs too much to replace an employee, so it's cheaper to do full vetting beforehand.

My nephew Ian went through four interviews for a job at a nonprofit organization. He so kindly gave me permission to use them in this book to show his strategy (although he did not use the double-hit method and just emailed the interviewers). He used a common template between each batch of letters (his second and third interviews both consisted of a pair interviewing him), including slight personal touches if he thought he had any good hooks. Mostly he wanted to emphasize his experience of dealing with the ebb and flow of work demands.

You'll find his emails below.

Hello Tammie,

Thank you so much for your phone call this morning. It was a pleasure to learn more about XXX, the workplace culture, and some of what I could be doing to contribute. I'm truly excited by the opportunity to join XXX and aid in your mission of returning people to stable housing and self-sufficiency. Working for a community-focused nonprofit is something I would find very personally rewarding, and I am sure that my skills and ability to learn new ones would be of use to XXX.

I look forward to hearing from Jaime on XXX's next steps. In the meantime, please do not hesitate to contact me if there is any additional information I can provide.

Best regards,
Ian McKee

Hi Erin,

Thank you so much for your time this afternoon at a very busy time of the year. It was great to learn more about XXX and what Data Development entails. It sounds like you are part of a great team that I would be happy to join. I really appreciated the "ground-level" view that you and Jaime provided, answering a number of my questions in addition to the ones I asked. Managing multiple data streams, having to prioritize responses, and dealing with seasonal "surges" are all facets of the work that I have experience with and would be glad to tackle again.

I'll be looking forward to the skill test and next steps in the hiring process. If you have any follow-up questions for me, please let me know.

Best regards,
Ian McKee

Hi Jaime,

Thank you so much for your time this afternoon at a very busy time of the year. It was great to learn more about XXX and what Data Development entails. It sounds like you are part of a great team that I would be happy to join. I really appreciated the "ground-level" view that you and Erin provided, answering a number of my questions in addition to the ones I asked. Managing multiple data streams, having to prioritize responses, and dealing with seasonal "surges" are all facets of the work that I have experience with and would be glad to tackle again.

I'll be looking forward to the skill test and next steps in the hiring process. If you have any follow-up questions for me, please let me know.

Best regards,
Ian McKee

Hello Tanya,

Thank you for taking the time out of a busy schedule to meet with me this morning. I understand that this is an exceptionally busy time of year for XXX and wish to apologize again for the scheduling mix-up.

I'm very appreciative of the information you and Carmen were able to share regarding the Data Development/DevOps teams. It sounds like the data doesn't rest idle for long, with much work to be done coordinating and targeting active campaigns; I would love to learn more about that actionable side of Data at XXX and how I might support it. I think my experience managing multiple incoming and outgoing data streams would be an asset for XXX, both in "normal" operations and during seasonal surges.

If you have any more questions for me, I would be happy to answer them at any time.

Best Regards,
Ian McKee

Hello Carmen,

Thank you for taking the time out of a busy schedule to meet with me this morning. I understand that this is an exceptionally busy time of year for XXX and wish to apologize again for the scheduling mix-up.

I'm very appreciative of the information you and Tanya were able to share regarding the Data Development/DevOps teams. It sounds like the data doesn't rest idle for long, with much work to be done coordinating and targeting active campaigns; I would love to learn more about that actionable side of Data at XXX and how I might support it. I think my experience managing multiple incoming and outgoing data streams would be an asset for XXX, both in "normal" operations and during seasonal surges.

If you have any more questions for me, I would be happy to answer them at any time.

Best Regards,
Ian McKee

As you can see, Ian used some repeated ideas for all of the letters but then got specific depending on what he'd talked about with each interviewer. He also called out his scheduling mishap, which he felt would make him seem more transparent and honest. These letters worked their magic because Ian is now employed there.

I checked with Robert W. Glass, Executive Vice President of Corporate Development with Robert Half International, one of the largest human resource consulting firms (with 345 locations worldwide). Were these post-interview notes no longer important? Bob Glass assured me his company was fully in favor of the Thank You note! He added there had recently been an opening in his company and that the person who got the job was the *only one* who wrote a note. In other words, knowing the field, culture, and expectations is key, but one can't lose when topping things off by sending a note.

Several students from colleges around the country approached me after a lecture I taught about thank you notes at a national conference in Michigan for Camp Kesem (a nonprofit with a free summer camp for children whose parents are dying or have died of cancer) student leaders. After my talk, young titans swarmed the podium. They revealed that what they are most afraid of upon graduating is not mastering the job itself but corresponding with clients to deepen the relationship.

In the modern job market search, younger people find this formal type of on-paper communication universally unpopular. At the time I was developing a curriculum to speak to UC Santa Cruz students about how to add the "soft skill" of writing to their job-seeking techniques. (Soft skills are character traits, emotional intelligence, and interpersonal skills that characterize a person's ability to effectively interact with others.) The head of Career Services told me something that made my jaw drop: He said many students are concerned that if they write a thank you or a personal note to a potential employer *before* they get the job, it will be perceived as "manipulative." Did I hear that right? When did taking advantage of a long-held practice of courtesy become *manipulative*?

And does sending a post-interview letter constitute "white privilege," that is, "the societal privilege that benefits white people over non-white people in some societies"? True, it's an expectation of the "white collar world," like a firm handshake, a business casual dress code, and the exchanging of business cards at networking events. Although it's estimated 26 percent of candidates write Thank You notes, some hiring managers weight this practice heavily. Does that give an advantage to candidates who learned how to compose Thank You notes over candidates who don't know how, don't want to, or blow it off as unimportant?

Jessica Liebman, Chief People Officer with technology blog Insider Inc., wrote what she thought was a benign article about how she takes thank you emails into account when she's hiring.[22]

She ruled that "not sending a follow-up often signals the person isn't actually interested in the role." She continued, "In a hiring process that's based on very few data points, it gives us the tiniest bit more data. The candidate is eager, organized, and well-mannered enough to send the note."

This ignited a firestorm of comments on the LinkedIn platform, including those who countered, "Sending a thank you note is an antiquated and pointless practice." Liebman disagreed. She disclosed that at Insider Inc., editorial applicants send Thank You notes after interviewing, *unprompted*. She posited that "most people ... still find the practice relevant."

Andrew Seaman, Senior Managing Editor for Jobs & Career Development at LinkedIn News, agreed with the validity of the post-interview thank you in his article "Should You Send Thank-You Notes After Job Interviews?"[23] He wrote, "One of the best arguments for sending thank-you notes is that it reminds people involved in the hiring process who you are among a sea of applicants."

Lack of Follow-Through

I was shocked to hear about candidates who skipped thank you notes! Make no mistake, not sending a Thank You will be the end of your candidacy for many hiring managers.

It's not the lack of courtesy (though that isn't a great sign either). Rather it's the perception of either disinterest or an inability to follow up.

If you won't take a few minutes to write an email after an interview, how interested can you be in the job? If you don't follow up with me, how can I trust you will follow up with colleagues or clients?

Ensure You Never Miss a Follow-Up with These Simple Tips

Tip #1: An email must be sent right away to everyone who interviews you.

"Right away" can be defined as twenty-four hours. If you need to take more time, make sure that email is well written.

Tip #2: A Thank You email can advance you to the next level.

It gives you an opportunity to reflect on the interview and reiterate details or rectify misinformation.

Tip #3: Don't just send a Thank You for the one interview. Send one for all interviews (like my nephew Ian did).

When sending multiple thank yous, take the time to personalize each letter for the experience you had with that person.

Tip #4: You don't need to handwrite—email is wonderful! Just make sure you don't procrastinate.

Handwriting is just not as acceptable anymore in a professional context, and we generally don't practice good penmanship. As a word here or there could be misread or misconstrued, you may want to err on the side of legibility versus flair.

Let's circle back to what Michael Seales said about "being authentic" in what you write. Just as I developed a cheat sheet of prompts to help you write a Thank You for a gift or service, I've also tried to break down what a solid set of cues would be for a post-interview email letter.

Now we are going to use the same template from your informal Thank You notes (the "Me, You, and Us" formula from Chapter Six) for your business follow-up letters.

Reflect back to the moment you learned the job was available and how excited you were because you were already familiar with the company and its work in the field.

ME:

1. "When I first learned about the position at your company, I had a solid sense that this was what I'd been hoping for ever since I was [young / in college / etc.]." (Only say this if it's true.)

YOU:

2. "You shed light on my questions, and your in-depth explanation of how [company name] works was enlightening. Thank you for your time today. I was inspired by hearing your story. I hope I, too, can one day make an impact on the company, just as you have."

US:

3. "Whatever the next steps in the hiring process may be, please know I'm eager to provide any additional information to help you decide."

Within the thank you, you can shoehorn in hints about your personality and work ethic and how you'd groove with the corporate culture. Describe how you're a decisive leader and a goal-oriented team player. Show you're an innovator by mentioning creative "wins." Be resilient and adaptable. Speak from the heart. Be your best self.

Now get ready to warm up your printer to write another Thank You the second you get the verbal job offer. Here you can mention the terms of your employment and your understanding of the terms of the offer itself.

It's time to send your freshly scanned, ready-to-mail letter on its way. Find the nearest safe mailbox—at the USPS local office, perhaps, or a secure box at your mother's real estate company. (Many neighborhoods are experiencing problems with criminals who steal outgoing mail. For that reason, to be super secure, I'm recommending using a guarded or protected mailbox rather than posting it out in front of your residence.)

Congratulations! You just got double exposure with your "first impression." A boss could easily delete your email, but when the same message in three-dimensional form arrives in a stamped envelope via snail mail a day later, it'll be more difficult for them to throw *that* away—or forget about you. In one dramatic example, a chairman of a major television network wrote me nine months after receiving my snail mail, apologizing for the long delay in responding but saying the letter was still on his desk. Soon thereafter, he and his wife gave their first unsolicited gift to the university I represent. Coincidence? I think not.

Letter Preparation

I use personalized stationery with my name and contact information on it so that a child could figure out where to respond to me. If I'm away from my desk and don't have my stationery nearby, I type something on the computer or typewriter and add an icon or mark to make people associate the paper with me (typewriters would be an obvious choice in my case). Voilà! No muss, no fuss, and free of charge. It's instant branding and cooler than a plain piece of white paper. It's also a bit of a tease about who you are, what drives you, and what style you have, providing the person in human resources another way to find or remember you. Don't you feel good when you receive an actual letter on real paper?

You don't have to create your own unique stationery, but it's not hard to do so. Find a customizable template and muck around with the font and colors you prefer and the positioning of your address and contact information. I'm giving you permission to have fun with it. Print it out to see how it looks in real life, off the computer screen. Check the colors to make sure they are what you want—sometimes the hue is off and doesn't translate off-screen, so review it for a "thumbs up" approval by the client (meaning *you* in this case).

Start your emails as you would a letter—that is, with the name of the person to whom you're writing—and include your own name at the bottom along with how to reach you. Properly capitalize the name of your (hopefully) future boss and the name of the company. Forget your easy, breezy way of communicating with your friends—like how you text back and forth with all lowercase letters and no periods or commas. That's fine for the purposes of casual interaction with friends and family. But this "looking for work" correspondence is more formal, so start sentences with capital letters and whip out your best punctuation.

You might consider creating your own stationery, perhaps using an app such as

Microsoft Create, to emphasize what you do or love. They say, for example, "If you own a dog grooming business, choosing stationery with dog paw prints running along the margins would add a nice touch." I've told musicians and sound mixers to add musical notes to their stationery or to use sheet music paper as the frame and glue their letter in the middle.[24] You don't need to do this, but it's another point of differentiation. Remember, finding a way to stand out is what this is all about!

Choose a cool font that represents your personality. Look online if none of the preprogrammed choices on your device thrill you. (I downloaded my favorite, American Typewriter, from a free font site.)

Next type your message on a Word document. Include the date so that it's right there as a time stamp if someone wants to print the letter out.

Speaking of printers, do you own or have access to one? An Epson printer/scanner goes for under $199. An HP wireless printer/scanner is even less—around $159—and arrives with two years' worth of ink included.

However you do it, print and scan your letter. Now it's time to email the message. Make sure your signature block has multiple ways to find you, including your email address, cell phone number, website, Instagram, and #hashtag.

Below is a fictitious example of a post-interview letter by email. Let's pretend I generated this in a quest for a "friend-raiser" job for Dean of the Arts at UC Santa Cruz. (It's true that a Banana Slug is the unofficial but beloved school mascot.)

- Notice that the letter is single-spaced.
- There are two lines after the inside address—the receiver's address—and the start of the actual letter. That block of information includes the name of the recipient, followed by the business title and company and snail mail address (if you have it) or email address. You'll put that on the upper left-hand side of your letter.
- Space down two lines before you begin your letter. The "Dear" is what I call the salutation, but don't feel obliged to remember that!
- After you've finished your letter, you may sign it in various ways depending on how close you feel to the person. If you have your own personal sign-off and it's not too informal for a business letter, use that. Some formal choices include:

  - Yours truly
  - Sincerely
  - Best wishes
  - Best regards
  - Warmly
  - All the best

I've received less-formal emails from friends who sign off as follows:

- Cheers
- Enjoy
- Hugs
- All my love
- Best
- Stay safe

There is one blank line after the "Yours truly" or "Sincerely."

- If you want to add a P.S., or postscript (in Latin, "postscriptum" means "written after"), leave several lines after the sign-off.

(Put today's DATE here) (Or put DATE here) (Two lines between inside address and "Dear")

Dear Ms. Smith:

Our meeting today about the "friend-raiser" job you and Dean Warburton created in the Arts Division made me even more enthusiastic about joining forces with my alma mater.

I've unofficially bragged about being a "Banana Slug" for years. This position would encourage me to meet fellow alums, parents, and recent graduates who share the same DNA—a love of UC Santa Cruz.

You get "two for one" with me. I've been on "both sides of the table." I understand the donor brain since I've supported Teach for America and Emerson College. I was on the Board of Trustees at Rhode Island School of Design, a private East Coast art school my daughter Jamie attended for fifteen years.

As a parent, I fervently believe students in the Arts need support. I would be honored to introduce Interim Dean Warburton to donors.

Alison, you mentioned a trip to Los Angeles for your son to test skateboard parks. I'll get you some recommendations.

Please pass along my thanks to Sarah Kudela for a great tour and even better overview. I'm extremely interested in the newly created Director of Special Projects position, and look forward to hearing from you soon.

Sincerely,

Erica Gerard Di Bona
(xxx) xxx-xxxx
(LinkedIn URL) (Website URL) #Hashtag
(If you wish, add your gender pronouns, such as she/her/hers, he/him/his, they/them/theirs, or ze/zir/zirs.)

After you've proofread the note three times and are sure there aren't any bonehead mistakes, you're almost ready. (Ask a friend or family member to eyeball it too.) Don't be too quick to hit "Send." Cite your name, phone number, blog or website info, hashtag, Instagram, and LinkedIn information in your email signature block. The more ways your future employer can find you, the better.

Here are some tips from the Yale Career Center on writing a Thank You after an interview:

First paragraph: Outline what you learned about the job itself and how it clarified your desire to become a part of an organization that does "such and such."

Second paragraph: Expand on what you liked about the scope of responsibility and what the interviewer specifically mentioned.

Second chance: If you didn't brag about some part of your background, use this as an opportunity to add a sentence and, if appropriate, attach relevant materials: "I know we didn't get a chance to chat in further detail about projects from my [insert title] class. I've attached a few of them here."

Last paragraph: This can be personal. If the interviewer mentioned an upcoming vacation, for example, recommend a favorite local restaurant in that area to circle back to your conversation. Convey you're very interested in the position and look forward to hearing from them soon.

Your coordinates—how to find you: Make sure to include your name, email, cell phone number, LinkedIn URL, website URL, and #hashtag, if relevant.

Send a follow-up note to each interviewer: If you've had several meetings across different interviewers, write separately to each of them. Tailor your comments to the conversation you had with each person. When interviewers compare notes, which they are sure to do, you won't embarrass yourself by having cribbed sentences from one letter to the other. This will prove you paid attention to what each person said.

While your letter should show gratitude, you still need to do the following:

- Reiterate your interest.
- Express your appreciation for the interviewer's time.
- Emphasize your best and most relevant qualities and skills.
- Mention a specific topic discussed in the interview that you found to be the most appealing.
- Include one or two past experiences that prepared you for the responsibilities of the position.

Here are a few methods to set yourself apart:

- Mention something exciting you learned about the company that makes you want to work there.
- Talk about a skills shortage you know the company has and how you're uniquely poised to solve that problem.
- Include links to projects or work samples you talked about in your interview.
- Comment on a small detail your interviewer mentioned (e.g., wish them safe travels if they said were going overseas for an upcoming vacation).
- Clarify something you said during the interview.
- Highlight something you failed to mention in the interview.

How Long Should I Wait?

You've heard a potential employer or recruiter decides who to hire within twenty-four hours of meeting, Zooming, or calling a candidate, so time is of the essence to catch that decision-making "sweet spot." If you wait more than a day or two to hit "Send" on your email, it may cost you the job. You also have twenty-four hours after the interview to get your act together. What does that mean?

During an in-person interview, did you meet with multiple levels of people at the company? Bad news—you should write each one their *own* letter. Don't cut and paste the same Thank You to everyone. There's a high probability the various interviewers will compare their received notes. Add something personal and pertinent that's germane to your interview in each individual letter. After you write your various notes, keep them for your own records in a big "scanned letters" file.

Maybe you didn't go for my snail mail approach, but you *did* send a grateful email quickly after the interview. You executed the scan and email followed by snail mail technique, if you had time. Otherwise, you at least sent the boss or human resources employee a grateful email right away so that you can beat out everyone else.

What happens if you blow it off? An interview Thank You email is considered the baseline of common courtesy in the job hunting market. It shows you're really interested in the position and want to win the job. An employer likes seeing that dedication. If you thought a follow-up Thank You wasn't necessary and didn't do anything, you run the risk of being seen as uncaring, uninterested, or even just plain rude.

You should use a professional tone, not a cutesy or folksy one-liner. Continue making the same positive impression you did in the interview. A note that's too short—such as

"Great to meet you yesterday, I look forward to hearing from you soon"—is a mistake. It's so generic that you're not giving any clues to the hiring folks about who the heck you are. You'll show up as less serious than your competing candidates. Similarly, an email that's laborious and too long is a turnoff. A few paragraphs is ideal. My nephew Ian said that he worked with five lines to get his point across.

What if you made a mistake in something you blurted out during the interview? Experts advise not to mention it in your follow-up email. Maybe the hiring team forgot about it or they didn't think it was a problem and you've been over-worrying. You run the risk of reminding them of your perceived gaffe and drawing more attention to it, so let it be.

But if you want to know what's going on, the trick is to find the right level of interest. Follow up but don't press. Respond quickly, send your email thanking folks for the chance to meet them, and then wait. Don't reach out after only one day has passed. Employers have a process they must go through before they can bring you (or anyone else) on board. Think about it—you're not the only job seeker around. They may be interviewing other candidates in addition to you or checking your references and then talking to other people in the company about whether you're a good fit. Don't send another email prematurely. If you're overeager, that can work against you too. You also should *not* use your Thank You note to ask about benefits, vacation time, salary, or the like. Your Thank You note has one objective— to show respect for the hiring team using the proper protocol.

Whatever you do, don't use your Thank You note as a way to beg. Just like on a date, it's a turnoff when someone seems desperate and overeager.

Now you must cool your jets and settle down for a few days to hear a response. However, if the boss said they needed to fill

> If you want to know what's going on, the trick is to find the right level of interest. Follow up but don't press. Respond quickly, send your email thanking folks for the chance to meet them, and then wait.

the position immediately, you can inquire after twenty-four hours.

If the interviewer promised to make a "warm introduction" for you (with someone in their network), give them two to three days to do it. Sorry to break it to you, but they have other things to accomplish besides trying to further your career!

It's also not appropriate or ethical to send a gift to the folks on the hiring team. It may be seen as trying to bribe them, and there are strict rules about gift giving when trying for a job. You might shoot yourself in the foot and

A puzzle gifted to Erica from
Cliff Selbert, ASLA, FSEGD.

A Visual Compendium of Typewriters

POP
CHART
LAB

500 pieces · 18" x 24"
Recommended for ages 5 and up

end up being disqualified from the pool of candidates, and that would be terrible.

If you sent your résumé to a blind ad on an anonymous website, it's probably sitting in Human Resources with hundreds of others. The staff needs time to read through what they've received. Don't be discouraged if you don't hear back. Unfortunately, not only ex-boyfriends can "ghost" you. Don't take it personally—you did your best. Kiss it off and move on. If that's their corporate culture, it might not be a fit for you anyway.

In "10 Mistakes to Avoid With a Job Interview Thank-You Email," U.S. News listed these **Thank You email faux pas:**[25]

- Waiting too long to send one
- Not sending one at all
- Following up too soon
- Using the wrong tone
- Making it too long or too short
- Apologizing for an interview mistake
- Asking about salary and benefits
- Begging for the job
- Making spelling mistakes
- Sending a gift

Now where do we stand on the topic of artificial intelligence (AI) taking over written language? As an old-school correspondent who uses a typewriter, I can't believe I am saying this, but as AI advances with content creator Chat Generative Pre-Trained Transformer (ChatGPT)—a "language model" designed to understand and generate human-like text—I would rather have you generate an AI Thank You card or letter than nothing at all. But will it have a personal touch?

If you specify what you want to say, the chatbot will compose it for you. My friend Betty Graham, a top realtor in Beverly Hills, tried it for a description of a house she wanted to list for sale, and she declared the

instant merging of intel she gave it combined with its own "brain" was better than what she could have put out. It will be interesting to see whether ChatGPT will eventually understand nuance or different customs. Will it realize Thank You notes are not "common courtesy" or "best practice" in all countries or communities?[26]

After putting all your work into finding the ideal job, applying for it, and then interviewing, why not go the extra nine yards and send the thank you card? Hopefully I have swayed you in the direction to take action! One caveat: If you're not qualified, a note won't get you the job, so it's not a miracle maker. And if you are applying for any and every job, I wouldn't send a thank you. Be focused on your heart's desire. I do hope to hear from you if you land a job where the thank you for the interview helped! ●

Chapter Eight

Standing Out Beyond the Thank You

A letter is a shapeshifter. While the thank you note itself has its own power, you can place other forms of messages in an envelope that also deliver value. In this electronic age, where it takes more ingenuity to capture someone's attention, finding a way to "get eyeballs" on yourself involves a return to basics. Don't reinvent the wheel—send your story in the mail!

You can modify the same letter writing technique you used post-interview to forge and develop personal and business relationships. It's a proven classic. A stamped letter in an envelope can be used multiple ways: to request a meeting, say hello, or simply acknowledge your interest in or appreciation for someone. Slow things down—offer someone a chance to *think* about you, and in so doing, you will stand out from those who are using only emails and texts to interface.

The techniques I rely on for starting relationships—using the USPS and a typewriter—have been successful tools for my work in development and fundraising. I spent thirty-five years in television production and met, interviewed, and hired hundreds of people, so I remember what kind of outreach caught my attention and what lost the gig for hopeful job seekers. Of all the forms of communication I have witnessed, letter writing wins. It's the superior way to build work relationships, procure meetings or interviews, start new friendships, and, ultimately, raise money for whatever organization you represent.

How to Build Personal and Business Relationships

Send a note of congratulations when someone you know has a win (i.e., their TV show got greenlit, they were promoted, or they were honored with an award). My special touch is to add clippings that substantiate the success. If I see a bus on the street with the name of the alum's movie or a billboard or bus stop with their picture, I've also been known to take a picture of it from my phone and text it. The producer or writer who sold that project is always delighted, and it's my own "Where's Waldo?" game I play. I also scout the entertainment trades and daily newspapers and magazines if I know the person is deeply interested in a certain topic—and it can be a running joke as mundane as "How hot is Lenny Kravitz?" to my girlfriend Donna or a serious investigation about financial divestitures at the university. You can forward the relevant info by email or text if you're not a paper-reading, magazine-clipping, playing-with-scissors person. We're all crazy busy, and only six out of ten adults read newspaper media each week.[27]

I know, I was surprised, too. That's before all the other forms of news and information that come at us on a daily basis, so it's easy to miss something.

Vin and I met multitalented comedian and actor Kevin Flynn through our friends Biff and Lynda Levy, who knew him from Boston and the Nantucket Comedy Festival (which he founded and for which they're long-time supporters on the board).[28]

Kevin wrote a one-man show called *Fear of Heights*[29] about choosing a different career than his father and grandfather, who were New York City ironworkers. There's an iconic black-and-white photograph called *Lunch atop a Skyscraper*,[30] credited to Charles C. Ebbets, featuring eleven guys seated on a beam stretching across the Manhattan skyline, feet dangling in the air sixty-nine floors up as they casually open their lunchboxes. Kevin's father is on that beam. I was so impressed with the incisive storytelling Kevin did to examine his own psyche and share about his Irish American upbringing that I wrote him a fan letter.

Congrats Letter

Reading an actual daily newspaper with its messy newsprint ink is not as popular as it used to be when I was growing up. Some people, like my sister-in-law Carol, are allergic to the smell of it, and the black ink is not friendly to white furniture.

If you don't subscribe to a daily chronicle, don't worry. A digital newspaper can also be "clipped," although, for me, it misses some of the

> Slow things down— offer someone a chance to think about you, and in so doing, you will stand out from those who are using only emails and texts to interface.

Happy birthday to Henry Winkler with horoscope.

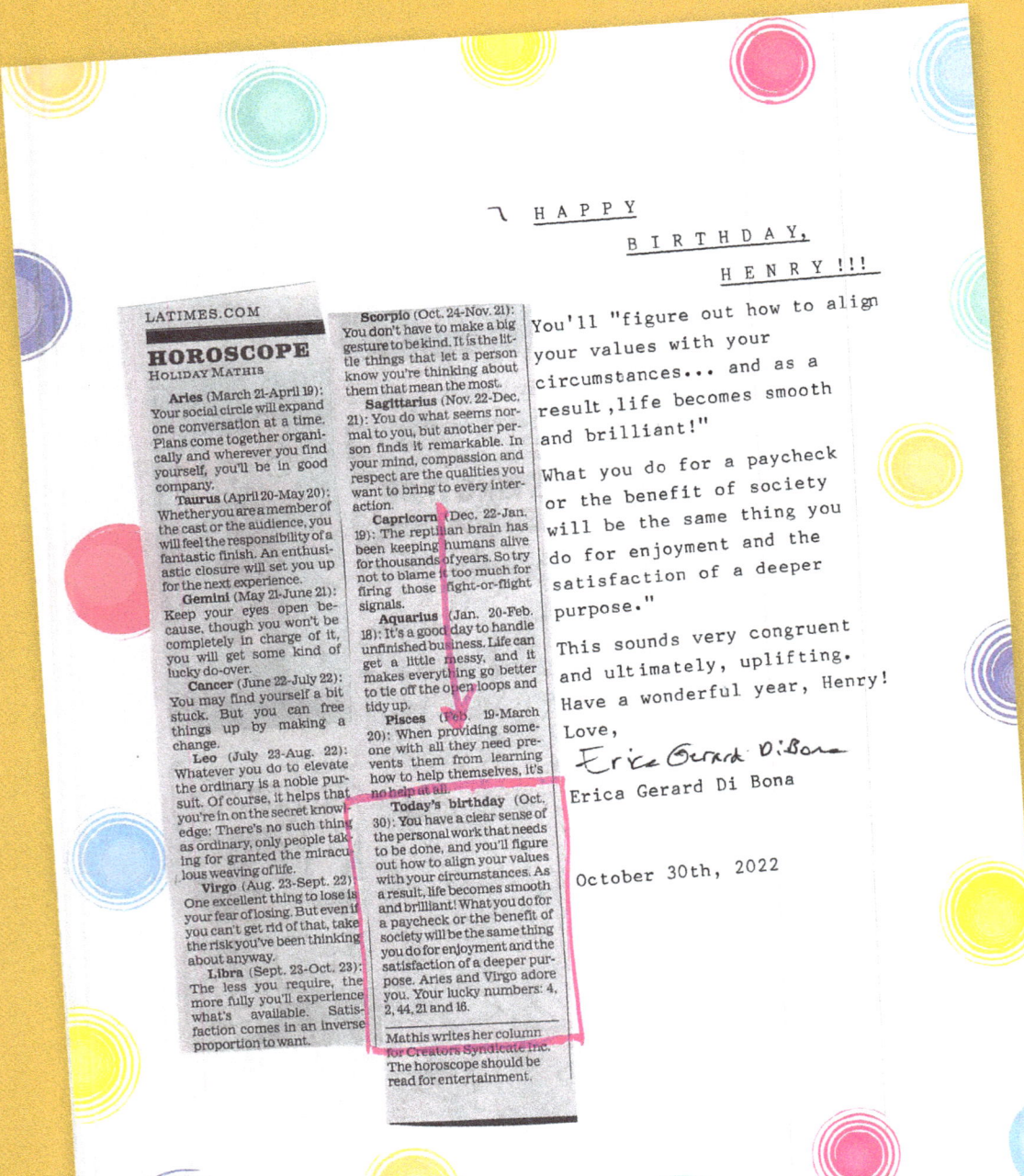

HAPPY

BIRTHDAY,

HENRY !!!

You'll "figure out how to align your values with your circumstances... and as a result, life becomes smooth and brilliant!"

What you do for a paycheck or the benefit of society will be the same thing you do for enjoyment and the satisfaction of a deeper purpose."

This sounds very congruent and ultimately, uplifting. Have a wonderful year, Henry! Love,

Erica Gerard Di Bona

Erica Gerard Di Bona

October 30th, 2022

LATIMES.COM

HOROSCOPE
HOLIDAY MATHIS

Aries (March 21-April 19): Your social circle will expand one conversation at a time. Plans come together organically and wherever you find yourself, you'll be in good company.

Taurus (April 20-May 20): Whether you are a member of the cast or the audience, you will feel the responsibility of a fantastic finish. An enthusiastic closure will set you up for the next experience.

Gemini (May 21-June 21): Keep your eyes open because, though you won't be completely in charge of it, you will get some kind of lucky do-over.

Cancer (June 22-July 22): You may find yourself a bit stuck. But you can free things up by making a change.

Leo (July 23-Aug. 22): Whatever you do to elevate the ordinary is a noble pursuit. Of course, it helps that you're in on the secret knowledge: There's no such thing as ordinary, only people taking for granted the miraculous weaving of life.

Virgo (Aug. 23-Sept. 22): One excellent thing to lose is your fear of losing. But even if you can't get rid of that, take the risk you've been thinking about anyway.

Libra (Sept. 23-Oct. 23): The less you require, the more fully you'll experience what's available. Satisfaction comes in an inverse proportion to want.

Scorpio (Oct. 24-Nov. 21): You don't have to make a big gesture to be kind. It is the little things that let a person know you're thinking about them that mean the most.

Sagittarius (Nov. 22-Dec. 21): You do what seems normal to you, but another person finds it remarkable. In your mind, compassion and respect are the qualities you want to bring to every interaction.

Capricorn (Dec. 22-Jan. 19): The reptilian brain has been keeping humans alive for thousands of years. So try not to blame it too much for firing those fight-or-flight signals.

Aquarius (Jan. 20-Feb. 18): It's a good day to handle unfinished business. Life can get a little messy, and it makes everything go better to tie off the open loops and tidy up.

Pisces (Feb. 19-March 20): When providing someone with all they need prevents them from learning how to help themselves, it's no help at all.

Today's birthday (Oct. 30): You have a clear sense of the personal work that needs to be done, and you'll figure out how to align your values with your circumstances. As a result, life becomes smooth and brilliant! What you do for a paycheck or the benefit of society will be the same thing you do for enjoyment and the satisfaction of a deeper purpose. Aries and Virgo adore you. Your lucky numbers: 4, 2, 44, 21 and 16.

Mathis writes her column for Creators Syndicate Inc. The horoscope should be read for entertainment.

homespun quality of a folded missile thrown onto your front porch. If the person you're thinking of doesn't peruse a newspaper carefully, they may miss information that could be helpful. I have curated information for friends and contacts who would have never seen a certain story otherwise, giving them intellectual fodder to contemplate.

Unfortunately, the newsprint newspaper and glossy magazines are dying models. I don't expect you to drive all over town to source newsstands that sell periodicals. It's easy to send an article via an email attachment or text, but I still prefer to snail mail a letter with a printed article or clipping inside for the most personal touch.

If it's a friend's or donor's birthday, I clip the horoscope from the *Los Angeles Times* to forecast what's ahead and tape or paste it to a fun, colorful piece of stationery. Then I scan and email it. The last step is to drop the printed version in the mailbox so that my friend or colleague can pin the prognostication to their bulletin board, if they even use one anymore. I saw Henry Winkler at the Emmys, and he thanked me for the horoscopes I cut out for him each year. My "Happy Birthday Horoscope" is corny and unusual, and I'm happy to provide good news, fabricated or not.

I am still old-school and keep a handwritten "birthday book." At the start of the month (or, if I'm really organized, at the end of the preceding month), I scan ahead to see whoever has an upcoming momentous occasion and transfer it into my online calendar. (Anniversaries and dates when a loved one died are also things I track.) Facebook is gratifying on birthdays, and some people joke that's the only reason they remain on that platform. It takes less than a second to click on a Facebook wish. Nice, but it hardly took any effort, you've gotta admit.

When you send someone an actual birthday card in the mail, you are one of a few people taking this action. You will stand out and be remembered. Plus it feels good to know someone is receiving a physical acknowledgment of their red-letter day because of you. Your card may end up in a file cabinet or a pretty box somewhere, which you can't say for a Facebook click.

Getting in the Door for a Business Meeting: Don't Give Up

In the entertainment world, "Development Hell" is when you've created or worked on a television show or film idea and then wait months to get to the meeting at which to sell it. You pitch your concept to a network executive and then stand by, fingers crossed, for a "yes" (greenlight) or "no." Vin proposed a Saturday morning kids' show called *Animal Crack-Ups* 136 times before he sold it. 136. If he can do it, so can you. His persistence and patience

Here's one of my most important insider tips: Appreciate support staff and let them know it—and, when possible, update their boss.

> **If you're attempting to reach someone to pitch an idea, product, business, or plan, a letter with a stamp provides you with another conduit.**

paid off. Everybody loves animals! The next time he went to sell a show, he sold it in the room with one pitch. *America's Funniest Videos* has been an ABC network staple for more than three decades.

Here's one of my most important insider tips: Appreciate support staff and let them know it—and, when possible, update their boss.

The administrative assistant or chief of staff is the all-mighty scheduler who can either ease you in to their boss's calendar or keep you out. As the assistant and I go through the tedious process of setting a meeting, I'll promise the admin, "When this is over, I'll tell your boss about what a great job you did." That promise will buoy the assistant's spirits because finding an agreed-upon date can be a long slog, with many changes along the

way. This is another area where persistence is imperative.

After we've "played calendar," I'll write the assistant a personal bravo about how I appreciated their help. Next time I call, the admin has received my letter and has a smile in their voice. After I meet the "top dog" (their boss), I write the chief executive about their wonderfully effective and protective assistant. I then send a *second* Thank You to the assistant who helped set it up, with a pointed "cc" at the bottom to their supervisor. The underling scheduler appreciates being complimented to the boss—and the letter will land in the assistant's Human Resources file, adding to their other plaudits. It may even help with a well-deserved promotion at some point. As the assistant rises through the ranks, you have established a stronger rapport than if you'd never taken the time to write a rave review about their help.

If you're attempting to reach someone to pitch an idea, product, business, or plan, a letter with a stamp provides you with another conduit. Sure, send your usual email, presentation, or text—but try sending snail mail too. It won't cost much and may render solid results. Have a problem that can't be solved? Write to the president of the company and see how quickly they respond. Just as you cozied up to the administrative assistant or chief of staff to get a meeting with their boss, you can similarly give a heads-up to the administrator who works with the CEO to be on the lookout for your letter. Now you have an advance team who cares about getting your message to the upper echelon. Go right to the top and stop wasting time with underlings who have no power to fix your problem.

It's harder now than it was before the pandemic to physically get everyone in the same room. Ever since COVID-19 forced everyone to work from home, we pivoted to meetings implementing video, audio, and chats because folks were trapped inside and production staff couldn't go on location. Online meeting apps exploded, including Microsoft Teams, GoTo Meeting, Google Hangouts, Cisco Webex Meetings, WhatsApp, etc. Production shoots and travel to other cities are now back on track, but remote Zoom-type video chats have become part of the landscape and a boon to setting meetings. Making friends with the gatekeeper has become more important than ever since odds are you can't stop by their cubicle and mooch a handful of candies from their crystal bowl while you schmooze. A Thank You is your best shot to put the gatekeeper in a better mood and put *you* in the fast-lane for meeting with the head honcho.

You can embellish your letter with a small gift if it's not improper and couldn't be considered any form of bribery. Some ideas include the following:

- Send a Starbucks gift card by email to that assistant for putting your call through. A gasoline card is always good, too, unless they drive an electric vehicle.
- Send a lottery ticket that they could win big on (it costs a dollar).
- Send a bookmark if you are trying to sell or recommend a book.
- Send a pop-open window card that displays a message when you open the front flap,[31] such as "Celebrating You," "Smile," "Be Strong," "Believe," "Thank You," "You've Got This," "Dream Big," or "Life is Beautiful."
- Send a cute (but not cloying) message card for when someone's kind words made your day or even changed your life.
- Send USPS postage stamps.
- Send an IOU for a lunch, drinks, coffee, or dinner.
- Send your business card if they don't already have it.

Outreach Works in All Fields

Walter Winchell, a Broadway reporter, drama critic, and journalist for the New York tabloids in the 1920s, said, "It pays to be nice to the people you meet on the way up, for they are the same people you meet on the way down."

You never know what will happen in show business. The tides of change are inevitable, and the friendlier you are to someone when they're struggling, the higher the chance they will be helpful when they're at the top of the food chain and *you* need *them*. It's not rocket science—it's good karma. So send a nice note to the gatekeeper when you can, but don't overdo it with gifts or flowers. (I have been known to ship See's Bridge Mix chocolates but usually for a colleague I already know.)

Folks in the television industry are often highly visual; they design sets, oversee the "look" of a show from costumes to lighting, and write colorful personality-driven characters and storylines. I try to catch their eye with an unusual approach. Sometimes I'll create a message on evocative notepaper. I pay attention to what USPS stamp I affix on the envelope, what color pen I use, what interesting flat objects I add (pop-open cards with "Be Happy," "You Matter," or "Thank You" are my current favorites). Sooner or later, my "prospects" take pity on me and agree to schedule a coffee meetup. If there's lag time from when they received my note to when they respond, I don't take it personally. It's an upper when someone I've been pursuing contacts me. The thrill of the hunt is what drives people like me who work in Development (and, before that, in television research). I've learned to be patient, which is difficult since I have Attention-Deficit/ Hyperactivity Disorder (ADHD). I am impulsive, act fast, and crave instant results.

> You can embellish your letter with a small gift if it's not improper and couldn't be considered any form of bribery.

The power of a Thank You has many applications. If you're a real estate broker, consider penning a note to your brand-new clients after they've agreed to let you represent their home. Don't wait until after you've closed escrow and the house has sold. Let the nervous buyers know immediately how pleased you are to work with them. This will start off the relationship on a good foot.

Expanding one's customer base works across all professions. In the medical and dental fields, if you've added a new patient to your roster, let them know you look forward to going on the healing journey with them. Sometimes it's scary to deal with health issues. Your reassurance of being a teammate will go a long way toward building trust.

If you're a physical or occupational therapist, let your new patients know you appreciate their letting you help them get stronger. Reach out if you teach Pilates, are a trainer in a gym, or work as a freelance masseuse. Your client will feel reassured about signing up for that expensive series of classes with you!

If you've just started with a new client who comes in for hair color or a haircut, thank them for trusting you with their locks. The same goes if you're a manicurist, a tattoo artist, a body waxer, or an eyelash affixer. (You can tell I live in Los Angeles!)

If you're an artist who recently had an opening at a gallery, thank the owner who promoted your work and the guests you invited (who hopefully bought your work) for their support.

Look around your life and see who could use a dose of gratitude. The more you generate, the more you'll receive.

Fundraising Letters

Everyone is always trying to fundraise for their favorite cause or organization: the local church, synagogue, or mosque; the soccer team; a politician; climate change; nursery school or college; or a Kickstarter campaign.

When an interested donor steps forward, asking for alms can be heavenly. It's pure joy when someone understands why I'm trying to get support for students and programs at UC Santa Cruz and agrees to donate.

If you are getting started in the networking game, you might have an ace up your sleeve that you don't recognize: If you attended college for two years (even if you transferred out), you're automatically part of the alumni network. Utilize that community. If there are classmate meetups, grab your printed business cards, brush your hair (unless you shave your head), and go! Work the room. A hint: If you stand by the bar, you'll catch more people because (a) everyone goes for a drink throughout the night; and (b) partiers near the liquor source tend to linger.

Play the "business card" game. The goal is to walk away with a pocket full of cards and then cull them to discern viable contacts. Now take the next step! Send a follow-up email within a day (twenty-four hours) to your new alumni

UNIVERSITY OF CALIFORNIA
SANTA CRUZ

GIVE. DON'T GIVE IN. THE CAMPAIGN FOR UC SANTA CRUZ

April 7, 2015

Dear Ken:

We were at UC Santa Cruz around the same time -- I was at KRESGE from '73 to '75. I transferred to UCLA and went into TV production. (Even interviewed Josh Taylor at DOOL for a show called "SOAP WORLD" produced by the King brothers). Everyone at your company was helpful and I remember thinking what a good culture there was on set. Now I know you were behind that!

I left TV a few years ago & went into 'friendraising' for the Arts & academia. When I met Dean David Yager from the Arts Division at UC Santa Cruz, I signed on -- he's the kind of visionary who dreams big and makes things happen.

I'd love to introduce you to him. It's the 50th Anniversary for our school, and David has a lot of compelling ideas on how to reach out from the redwoods to Southern California.

Could we book a half-hour of your time when Dean Yager's in town? He'll be here:

    * Monday, April 27th
    and
    * Tuesday, April 28th

I'm working with Lesley Brander, and you've tried to make a visit happen before, but you got ill and it slid off the books, she said. For old times' sake -- and for the fact that my birthday's a day before yours (June 15th) and my mother's also named "Betty" -- can we set something up? I'd love to meet you!

Best,

Erica Gerard Di Bona
Kresge '73 to '75/Director, Special Projects

1156 High Street, Santa Cruz, CA 95064 | www.UCSC.edu

Fundraising letter
to Ken Corday.

"friend" before they forget who you are and how you met. Keep the momentum going. What do they say? "The early bird gets the worm."

On the opposite end of the "one-hit wonder," where the donor gives money the very first time you meet them, is the more plodding "donor journey." This refers to how you slowly build rapport with a potential donor, keeping the new interaction alive while you determine (a) if they are interested in giving and, (b) if so, how much and to what specific cause, and then (c) translate their dreams into reality as an Advancement officer, and (d) help them give to whatever program, professor, scholastic division, materials fund, or infrastructure is meaningful to them.

My approach to the donor journey requires careful tending because my goal is to move the potential philanthropist from "somewhat aware" to "fully committed." Sometimes an alum is pissed off about not being reached out to before, feeling ignored, or not being honored. There's a great deal of customer service involved in what any development officer does. There is a theory that one should expect to reach out at least seven times in different ways to engender one response. These "touches" or reach-outs may seem heavy-handed, but remember, you're trying to bring the unhappy person back into the fold. A magazine or newspaper clipping, either sent electronically or on paper, is one way to connect because it's lighthearted and also lets them know you are thinking of them. After a while, if I've played it right, I feel their resolve dissipate, and a renewed interest in their alma mater emerges.

My challenge is to entice a stranger to a meeting—and it's as hard as gaining the confidence of a solitary and elusive snow leopard. First, I build trust. A mighty beast won't approach a stranger, and similarly, a donor won't lean my way until they feel safe. Sophisticated folks realize a development or advancement officer will ultimately ask for money, help, or services. My challenge is to be authentic, the same way my

> Every time I create an outreach, before I roll it out of the typewriter carriage, I ask, "If I received this, how would I respond?"

father taught me to "find something nice to say about the boy."

When I'm figuring out how to procure a donor meeting, I wear two hats. As someone who has been a donor *and* become a development officer, I have the advantage of being able to guess what might attract someone's attention—and what won't. Every time I create an outreach, before I roll it out of the typewriter carriage, I ask, "If I received this, how would I respond?" I hope my message is intriguing, genuine, and makes the recipient smile because it's typed.

Spreading Kindness One Note at a Time

A billboard that caught my eye had former President Abraham Lincoln's famous phrase on it: "A house divided cannot stand." Underneath was the phrase "Civility: pass it on." I smiled to myself because I've always hoped my notes might introduce kindness into a strife-filled world. Letters and thank you notes add gentility wherever they go—to a classroom, a boardroom, or even the grocery store.

On one board I was on, tension ran high when I first joined, so the chairman and I cooked up what we dubbed a "civility campaign." I began sending "good job" notes to my fellow trustees, along with nice Museum of Modern Art three-dimensional holiday cards with special observations about what each person's insights added to the meetings. When a trustee had concluded their time commitment, I wrote them a note saying, "Thank you for your service, you've made a huge difference," and had it signed by all the other board members. Folks felt appreciated and seen. Gradually, we saw people's defenses drop, and kindness infused the formerly tense environment. I like to think the personalized "thanks for being you" letters enabled that pivot and helped create new collegiality.

Civility campaign letter: A "thanks for being you" stealth civility campaign can warm up the room and reassure formerly antagonistic colleagues you "mean them no harm," as my father would say. The frosty folks may relax their shoulders, drop their defenses, and become inquisitive about you or, at the very least, appreciate what you've accomplished with your "kindness caravan." The world is full of sticky situations that have gone south and created distrust between people. Here's a chance to cement a new relationship or rebuild a broken friendship using words, not weapons. What's that expression Vin's late mother, Jean, loved? "The pen is mightier than the sword."

Now that we have covered the more positive and joyous parts of thank yous and letter writing, we take a bit of a turn to the more somber aspect of correspondence in the next chapter—the condolence. ●

There is a theory that one should expect to reach out at least seven times in different ways to engender one response.

Chapter Nine

Condolences

Death is scary. Most of us don't know what to say or do around a person who's on their way out and may avoid visiting them in their last days because it's so difficult—and final. When our friend or family member is then gone, we're similarly adrift about what to say to their loved ones. What words could we possibly speak that would provide comfort? We don't know how to help, so we prefer to be polite and "give them space," but in doing so, we are absent and silent when our friends need us the most.

Ironically, trying to be polite and doing nothing renders us the most *impolite* we could be at a critical time in our friend's life. A lesson plan in grieving does not exist. There is no right way to address grief, as it varies for everyone, except to acknowledge what happened, say how much the person meant to you and to your friend, and be present for your friend if they need you. There is no wrong way—except to pretend the death *didn't* happen and avoid saying anything at all to the person who lost a loved one.

In a college linguistics class I learned that the more important a concept is in a culture, the more words exist to describe it. (Think of how many alternative descriptions there are for money, types of snow in Alaska, and female or male sexually oriented body parts.) It's the same rich treasure trove of synonyms regarding the final milestone—or should I say headstone? There are at least thirty-six synonyms for death, including the following: cessation, curtains, demise, end, euthanasia, extermination, extinction, finis, finish, necrosis, oblivion, release, repose, termination, decease, end of life, passing, afterlife, eternal rest, final rest, final sleep, passing over, exiting, ceasing to live, and transition. Some humorous ones are kicking the bucket, biting the dust, buying the farm, and cashing in one's chips. Religiously oriented terms include going to glory, going to one's reward, and meeting one's maker.

In our conversations and condolence card writing, we skirt around the "D" word—*death*. Are we afraid we might trigger our friend or family member by reminding them of what just happened? We don't want to upset them by pointing out the new reality, an empty chair at the holiday table. Or are we afraid of triggering ourselves instead? Isn't it obvious the person isn't with us anymore?

Truth is, *the person died.* There is no getting around it. If you're too squeamish to say that

> Ironically, trying to be polite and doing nothing renders us the most impolite we could be at a critical time in our friend's life.

directly in your condolence letter, you can find many other options rather than venture into the heart of darkness.

You don't need to make the survivor feel better about the situation. There is no solution for helping someone get through their grieving pain free. You need to show empathy and let them know they are in your heart and in your thoughts. **I say go for the D-word.** That person knows their loved one died. If they are that emotionally fragile, there is no helping them. I don't think there is anything wrong with saying the word "death" in your correspondence. So say, "I am sorry to hear your grandmother died," versus "passed or "transitioned." (Of course, if you have thanatophobia, an intense fear of death or the dying process, you're excused from writing a condolence.) Thanatophobia can be treated with Existential Psychotherapy, or Cognitive Behavioral Therapy (CBT). Talk about your psychological paralysis with an expert.

Sending a sympathy card shows you care and you're thinking of the person. If you don't suffer from a crippling fear of writing condolences phobia (is there a term for that?), I know you can summon up the internal fortitude to compose a meaningful note to someone who lost a friend, parent, or beloved pet. The greeting card industry makes cards for animal owners, too, which is wonderful. I've stocked up, as many of my friends have cats or dogs who are beloved family members and, like my friends, are getting older by the day. The term used to describe a pet's death in a comforting way is "crossing the Rainbow Bridge."

Be Mindful of the Purpose of Your Condolence

When writing a condolence, I take a few minutes to think about what that person meant to me and try to recall any stories that symbolize who they were—a tidbit about their sense of humor, their zest for life, or their favorite places, pastimes, or hobbies.

In the case of my dermatologist's father, I watched how carefully my doctor had looked out for his parents over the years, including frequent trips back East and then moving them to California where he found the best retirement home so that he could visit them more often. So when I wrote my doctor the condolence for their death, I included what a devoted son I knew him to be and how proud his father must have been of his son's thriving practice.

You can send a card even if you went to the funeral, but it's especially important if you couldn't get there and want the family to know how you felt about the deceased. When my sister Kitty died after a protracted battle with breast cancer, six hundred people attended her funeral in Palo Alto, California. Many friends couldn't attend, though, and condolence cards flooded in for weeks. I'd forgotten how popular we were as a family, and it was comforting to see my late sister being remembered. I lined up the cards as they came in (and this was over twenty years ago, when condolence cards were still popular), and that lineup brought me peace. Many people shared memories of an experience they'd had with Kitty, and I heard shards of the past I'd never known about.

It becomes a Rorschach test to posthumously piece together all the various parts of your loved one's personality from different points of view. In so doing, you remember things you'd forgotten, learn things you'd never known before, and create a bigger picture of the one you lost.

Other Reflections On The Deceased Can Include The Following

Were they into sports?

Were they a creative chef, baker, or hostess who loved throwing Christmas parties or feeding friends and family?

> You can send a card even if you went to the funeral, but it's especially important if you couldn't get there and want the family to know how you felt about the deceased.

Were they proud of their hometown, college, or any particular city, state, or country they'd visited or lived in?

What pops up when you run a mental scan of their likes and dislikes?

All this reflection can be woven into the correspondence as well as offers to be there to listen any time of day or night. If you mean it, tell them you'll check in on them and follow through. This is not a time to flake. Be present.

Taboos of Condolence Etiquette

What not to do is offer, "I know what you're feeling," or give unsolicited advice. You *don't* know what they are going through, and everyone has their own way to process grief.

Also, skip the stories about your *own* losses. They aren't equivalent, and this isn't a "who can top whom in grief" game. This is a time for support.

Sending a text is not enough when offering condolences. It's far too impersonal and requires the recipient answer it immediately—which is the opposite of how the mourner may be feeling. Often people want to be left alone until they can deal with communicating or choose their times for social interaction. It could be weeks before they feel up to responding. Don't be angry if you don't hear from them right away. They may not be in town or might have taken bereavement leave for a few days right after the family member died. Maybe they're dealing with making funeral arrangements, contacting their own family members or work colleagues, or going through the dead person's house or belongings to see what needs to be done next (e.g., to distribute items per the will or prepare to sell the property).

Be gentle with your friends who have sustained a loss. Don't expect them to be on *your* timetable. They've entered a land of their own, which experts say may take anywhere from six months to four years to navigate.

Alternative Condolences

Remember, condolences are not only about telling the mourner you're sorry—they're also a

> Remember, condolences are not only about telling the mourner you're sorry—they're also a way to process your own grief.

way to process your own grief. When you first learn the person has died, you may be sad and experience your own way of mourning. If it's your loss, too, find ways to reflect on how that person affected you and take time to connect with your own emotions. Just as I suggest not writing a Thank You until you've had time to reflect on and admire the gift you received, this is also a moment to stop, think, and then write. You may feel the need to say goodbye in a symbolic way if you weren't able to get there in person or didn't know the person was dying or if it was a sudden, unexpected tragedy.

When I learn someone has died, I light a candle that evening, shoot a video on my phone for the person who is grieving, and say a prayer. For Jews, this is a Yahrzeit candle, lit in memory of the dead. You can buy one made by Manischewitz, the same company that produces sweet kosher grape wine showcased at holidays. These "twenty-four-hour" candles burn for up to twenty-six hours and are ignited before sundown. This custom is also used as a remembrance on the anniversary of the death according to the Jewish calendar.

As someone who converted to Judaism as an adult and didn't grow up with Jewish traditions, I'm not as bound by custom as I probably should be—I do it my own way. I don't use a Yahrzeit candle unless I have one in the house. (As I wrote this, I just ordered a four-pack to test their burn time.) Anything that smells nice and is long-lasting feels appropriate. I record a video of the candle as I light it and send it to the mourner and then send another progress report video as the candle burns.

For me, the flickering fire signifies that the dead person's spirit is nearby. Often the memorial candle lasts several days, which gives me a way to say a protracted goodbye. I feel a closeness whenever I look at the wick dancing with the flame, and by sharing the video with the mourner, they know that they're not alone, although I'm not physically there. They are reassured that another person also acknowledges the transitioning of a beloved mortal or animal, if you wish, to the other side. When the fire is out, I sense the soul has ascended to another sphere.

Tributes

In addition to lighting a memorial candle, you can create more enduring tributes. You can support an organization the person loved or start an event to fundraise for a cause they cared about and then donate the proceeds in your friend's name. If they died of ovarian or breast cancer, you can contribute to research for a cure. If you make a donation, writing your condolence becomes easier because the helpful act stands for itself. If a nonprofit organization helped extend the deceased's life or saw them through to the end, you can bequeath funds to that place (think St. Jude's, a hospital, or a medical research center). My late father, a chemist, believed each year that passes gives us new medical breakthroughs, and he always stressed that research money is the foundation for hope.

You could also fund a scholarship in your friend's or family member's name at their college, give to the high school's football team, or donate to the local library. Put together a GoFundMe campaign for the family if the person died of tragic and unexpected circumstances and left their loved ones financially strapped or unable to pay for the funeral.

If you are on a food train for "sympathy meals" at the house of the grieving family, include a note with what you brought explaining what the food is, what ingredients are in it, and how to reheat it. You can add a few extra words of support too.

The condolence letter is your first outreach, but it doesn't have to be the only time you connect. If you have any tribute ideas in mind, you can certainly tell the person who lost their family member or friend what you're planning to do. You can work on your own to start your project

and then regroup after the fact to let the mourner know what you did and how it went. This gives you another chance to establish contact and give the grieving family continued courage.

The "ME, YOU/THEM, and US" Structure for Condolences

So, what to say? The formula for writing a condolence note is basically a variation of the three-paragraph "Me, You, and Us" format of the Thank You note. You can start with the word "when" if you wish—it's always a good way to immediately draw in your audience.

A few words and phrases come up as suggested language for condolences. They all seem rather interchangeable, so don't feel locked in by them—you can be creative. Rather than make you create different scenarios for how to react to a lost colleague, sibling, parent or grandparent, or friend, I'm going to give you a cheat sheet, from which you can pick and choose the phrases that apply. One thing I do to get psyched to write a condolence is similar to part of my process before I thank someone for a present: I immerse myself in thoughts of the person before I put pen to paper. I try to come up with a story about them, a unique characteristic they had, or a moment we shared.

In this case, the "Me" explains how you felt when you heard the news. You can still use the trigger word "when" as a prompt or bridge to structure the sentence in the condolence. Also, "when" can be used to get yourself thinking of how you reacted when you heard the news.

- When I heard [insert name] was gone...
- I was devastated when I learned of your grandmother's passing. I'd always hoped she would live forever. She had enough love to share with our entire neighborhood.

- **When** I learned you lost your brother, my heart broke for you, and I knew immediately that life without him would never be the same.
- It hit me hard **when** your mother died. She was an important part of my childhood, and I remember many afternoons when I'd bike over to your house after school and your mom cared almost as much about how *my* day was as she did about yours! She was my second mother, and I appreciate your generosity in letting me share her attention.
- I am so grateful you let me know **when** your father was ill and that I was able to see him one last time. That visit meant the world to me, and I'll always remember how he told me, "Don't let anyone take away your smile." He faced the world with his positive attitude, and his optimism shed light over many dark situations and encouraged me to do the same.
- I still laugh **when** I think about [something funny they did] or the time [an event you and the person shared].

The **"You/Them"** is about the relationship between your friend the mourner (**"YOU"**) and the person who died (**"THEM"**). This is where to connect the person you're writing to with your memories or stories of the person who's gone. For example: "I remember how if you were at a restaurant, you always encouraged your cost-conscious grandfather to order filet mignon if it was on the menu and not look at the price! After a while, we smiled when he went right for it."

You can also be helped by the answers to "what" and "why" questions:

- Your father meant so much to me. (Why?)
- He was the first person to ever …. (What?)
- He had the best advice. I'll always remember when he told me, "If you're driving to work thin-lipped and bitter, maybe it's time to find another job." Soon after that, I did.

- He had the best jokes (the corniest and dirtiest, too, but he was so cool he could pull it off).
- He baked the best chocolate chip cookies—better than at any bakery! He used Ghirardelli chocolate, which was the highest quality available, and doubled the amount of chips so every bite was gooey and delicious.
- He brought light and happiness to so many with his eternal optimism.
- There was only one [name] and I'm so grateful I had the chance to know him.
- I can still hear him saying, "There's always time to panic later"—his favorite phrase.
- I can still taste his bouillabaisse. He claimed it was "the best this side of Marseilles," and he was right! Nobody will ever duplicate his super garlicky rouille or his joy in feeding people. We didn't dare turn down a bite because it was his way of showing love.

With **"US,"** you can proceed from here as a supportive friend.

- I've walked down this road when my parents both died and know how much is involved in closing out a person's life.
- If you need help searching for paperwork, curating closets, or designing the proper memorial, sadly, I have experience in all those areas.
- I'm here for you, and please lean on me.
- You don't have to take this all on by yourself.

Don't worry about making a mistake in what you say. The biggest mistake is to not say anything and let your friend or family member think you don't care. Words themselves aren't as important as conveying the overarching sentiment of "I love you," "I'm thinking of you and miss the person too," and "I'll be there for you in any way I can" (if you mean it).

(For the sake of consistency, all of the phrases refer to "he"/"his.")

Phrases that pay (YOU)
So sorry for your loss.
Sending healing prayers and warm hugs.
Wishing you comfort and peace.
We will keep you and your family in our thoughts and prayers.
Thinking of you in this difficult/trying time.

Phrases for how you are reacting (ME)
I'm sorry/saddened/deeply saddened/stricken/devastated to hear about [name's] passing/death.
I'm grateful I got to know him and be part of your family.
His impact on my life is a tribute to his beautiful soul/shining spirit.
He did so much for his community/church/college/family, and his legacy will continue.
Your [loved one] meant so much to me. I still laugh when I think of [when he did something funny] or when I think of the time that [whatever it was].
There was only one [name]. There will never be another like him.
He was the first person to encourage me/tell me/teach me [whatever it was].
He had the best advice.
He had the funniest/corniest jokes.
He had the best ideas about travel/restaurants/real estate/investments.

Going forward (US)
You're not alone. I'll be there for you day or night, so please text or call whenever you need to hear a supportive voice.
I have started a fund in his name at his college [or whatever else you did to honor him]. I'll tell you more about it as it evolves and grows.
May you find strength in the shared memories and his spirit guide you through the challenging days ahead.
The first few months are the hardest, I found, and although life goes on, it's never quite the same.
[Name] will always be a part of your story, and all he's taught you and showed you will continue to guide you. Even though he's not here in person—he's in your heart.
His time here was far too short, but his impact was immeasurable.

It gets trickier if there was a fractured or tense relationship between parent and child—obviously don't mention that friction in the letter. You can say something like, "I know your relationship wasn't always easy to navigate, and I hope you can be gentle on yourself as you deal with this momentous shift."

A Famous Figure Many Called a Friend

When *Friends* star Matthew Perry was found deceased, I immediately thought of our friend Kevin Bright, who was the Executive Producer and Director of that series for years. There was a letter in the newspaper to "Ask Amy" from a fan, "Hurting in California," who admitted feeling gutted at his death. *(See next page.)* Since I'd never seen a question like that before, I cut it out and included it to Kevin as part of my condolence. He added a postscript—"And now Norman is gone"—in reference to producer-writer-director Norman Lear, another person he had collaborated with, who had just passed at age 101.

Elderly Friends

I met Doris and Bernie Nemtzow in Newport, Rhode Island; they were friends of Vin's mother and well known in the city. Doris and I became pen pals, even after they moved to Florida. She gave me a necklace of gold typewriter keys and a typewriter that had been in their closet for years. Bernie passed unexpectedly, and Doris was devastated. They'd been married for more than seventy years. I continue

---

Erica Gerard Di Bona

10293 Century Woods Drive, Los Angeles, California 900

September 9, 2023

Ms. Doris Nemtzow

Dear Doris:

The Synagogue sent out the notice that Bernie had died, and I sat at my computer for quite some time, staring at the screen and hoping it was not what I had just read.

Bernie always seemed like he would live forever. The two of you were ying and yang, the two halves of a perfectly formed seashell, each complementing and supporting the other.

Bernie had a perennial twinkle in his eye and was obviously as much in love with you as the day you met -- if not more. He had a jump in his step when I saw you both in Newport, and he was schlepping large boxes to the Post Office when you decided to move to Florida full-time, and I marveled at how strong he was. It must have been all those years of tennis-playing, I decided. He had the determination and initiative that he must have had as an executive back in New York, when the two of you were going to galas and Presidential Inaugurations (!) and social-hopping as you built your 'brand'.

Later, you shared your anniversary with the entire city of Newport, so that families could all enjoy the ocean on your special August 13th day. Bernie and you shared philanthropy, too, which also bound you in good karma.

I sent a donation to the Synagogue, and hope it finds its way to the right department. It seemed appropriate that Bernie's final impact would be to continue to give to the city you both loved. I will miss your husband, Doris. I will listen to whatever memories you want to share, and know that we will keep his name on our tongues as we speak about who he was as a man, an honorable man, a wonderful father and a husband for the ages. I am so sorry for your loss.
Love, Erica Di Bona

Check out my blog: ArtofThankYou.com

Condolence letter to Doris Nemtzow.

Erica Gerard Di Bona

November 18, 2023

Mr. Kevin Bright

Dear Kevin:

In all the time I've been reading advice columns --
and it's been basically since I was a kid -- I have
never seen someone write in about their grief for a
cultural figure...

and this person is obviously hurting as you are about
the loss of Matthew Perry.

*
It's been a tough time, with some really bright lights
suddenly dimmed. Vin still has a photo of Bob Saget
next to his computer and he looks at him daily. I'm
sure you have many, many memories of your time with
Matthew, and hope that the happy moments will sustain
you through the sadder times.

Your dedication to Emerson College is to be singled out.
The fact that you went to Boston for a Board meeting
right after getting this very sad news speaks to how
much you appreciate your alma mater and how much you
care about the next generation... although there will
never be another talent like your friend.

Love,

Erica Gerard Di Bona

Check out my blog: ArtofThankYou.com

From The Los Angeles TIMES "Ask Amy" column
of Saturday, November 18, 2023

ASK AMY

Sad over loss of a 'Friend'

Dear Amy: I've been in a bad place, and I'm a little surprised at the reason: I am grieving over the death of Matthew Perry.

I couldn't identify why I was feeling so low, until I finally realized that what I was feeling was grief.

How can you grieve someone that you never knew personally?

I think maybe it has to do with what I felt this person gave to me. I just wish I could say, "Thank you for all the laughs!"

What is your perspective on this type of thing?

HURTING IN CALIFORNIA

Dear Hurting: As of this writing, the death of this beloved actor is very new, and I can well understand why you (and many others) feel real grief over this loss.

Actors, musicians, writers and other cultural figures can make an indelible mark on our own real and lived experience. When the loss involves an actor who created a memorable character who came into our living rooms over such a long period of time, you feel as if you have lost a real "Friend."

Perry's decades-long and very public struggle with addiction adds a tragic poignancy to the end of his life, which came way too soon.

Reading accounts of the extreme physical consequences of his alcohol and drug addiction, as well as his many painful, heartbreaking and public relapses, one realizes that fame, fortune and the very best Friends were ultimately no match for this disease.

Perry knew he'd be remembered for "Friends" but wished he would be remembered for his role in helping other addicts on the road to sobriety. Many people in recovery have spoken about his vital role in personally helping them, including his choice to turn his former home into a sober living facility called the Perry House.

His death is a legitimate loss to mourn, but also a legacy to celebrate.

to write Doris, who just celebrated her one-hundredth birthday and sent me pictures of herself kicking her legs up in the air—her zest for life continues despite her frailty and loss.

Final Letters

My ex-husband Josh called me the "Angel of Death" and joked, "Don't send me any letters if I'm sick," because I'd been the final correspondent for *many* people at the end of their days. I laughed when he said it, but I didn't think it was all that funny. Truth is, I wasn't targeting seniors or trying to be the Grim Reaper, but since I was already pen pals with older people it made sense mine would be the last letter they would receive.

One time I wrote Camille Parolisi, a well-known former restaurant owner in Providence, Rhode Island (her place was appropriately named Camille's), and I knew she was struggling health-wise. By now she was 102. I was on the freeway driving home after seeing a friend when Vin called.

"Camille died," he announced.

I had reached out a few days before, and her niece had reported "Auntie" wasn't doing so well and couldn't come to the phone, so I said I'd write a letter instead. As I continued down the busy San Diego Freeway, I suddenly realized what Vin's news meant: My snail mail letter was still traveling cross-country—and Camille would never read it. It was strange to know it would never be seen by its intended recipient.

Similarly, years before, I'd sent my grandfather one of the weekly letters we'd swapped my entire life. He had cancer, and my mother and I had traveled up to Seattle to say goodbye. As we sat in the hospital room, I saw a familiar-looking envelope on his gray hospital tray. It was a letter from me. Choking

Sometimes a Thank You becomes "thank you for giving me the life and values you did."

back tears, I read it to him, knowing this was our final exchange. I was grateful I could say those words to him. I knew as I recited them that he would never write a rejoinder.

Sometimes a Thank You becomes "thank you for giving me the life and values you did."

My mother and I were never close, but I had maintained a sense of a relationship by sending clippings to her over the years. She'd trained as a journalist during World War II, and we had the same interest in news and newspapers. I didn't need to share intimacies about my life because that wasn't the space we'd cultivated. But I created enough of a connection that when she passed, I felt like I had made an effort to be a good daughter and hoped she knew I loved her.

When it became evident the end was imminent, I didn't know what to say as she faded away, and she couldn't get on the phone anymore. So I seized on an idea: It was near Thanksgiving, and I would write her a Thank You for everything she'd taught me. It's always easier for me to write emotions down than to say them out loud, and we'd never had a chatty relationship, so she wouldn't have expected that type of communication from me anyway.

I drafted a typed, single-spaced, two-page missive and inserted it into an envelope along with a three-dimensional card of a turkey carved from balsa wood. When my sister Annie told me to get up to Palo Alto—and quickly—I was charging out the front door when I remembered my letter was in the mailbox. I grabbed it, and when I arrived at my mother's house, my sister said I should go to the bedroom right away. I really wasn't prepared for instant action. I was scared and asked if I could wait until morning, but the hospice nurse and my sister agreed my mom didn't have that long.

The "Me, You, and Us" condolence letter I'm urging you to write is intended for those who remain on Earth after their family member or friend has passed.

I tiptoed into her darkened room. Shaking, I read the letter out loud, much like I'd orated to her father—my grandfather—years before. My mother didn't respond; she was past verbalizing. The room was quiet except for her labored breathing, but I imagined she could hear me, or at least I hoped she could. I finished the letter, kissed her, and quietly left. Twenty minutes later, she was gone. I don't know if she waited for me or if my message validated her role as my mother, and I'll never find out. I'd said what I needed to say. It was my final "thank you for being you" to the woman who instilled the importance of writing Thank You notes in all of her children.

For me, a condolence is the final "I see you and appreciate you" on the continuum of correspondence. Throughout our lives, we let each other know how much we mean to each other, and personal letters enhance that communication. Call me the Angel of Death if you will, but I *have* sent a lot of people what became their final piece of mail. I hope you agree that a life lived with recognition from those around us is a happier existence than being alone and unseen.

Letter writing is a permanent way to show attention, affection, and care. I enjoy writing people of all ages, and sometimes it so happens I've mailed the last envelope they ever receive—mostly because nobody else was doing it. There has been a silver lining to this faithful habit: I count myself grateful I could express my feelings to both Granddaddy Al and my mother as they took their last breaths. What is more holy than that? It is not communion but communication.

If your friend or family member is a total curmudgeon who has trouble showing and accepting emotion, they are the exception. For most of us, expressing love for one another is something we always desire, no matter how old or feeble we become. We crave receiving and giving love. So as we approach our "expiration date," it makes sense that we would want to continue receiving adoration and accolades—especially if we *know* our time is short.

The "Me, You, and Us" condolence letter I'm urging you to write is intended for those who remain on Earth after their family member or friend has passed. It's a chance to story-tell about that departed person, how they affected you, and what mark they left on their community or the world. You can help them patch together a Rashomon of untold sides of their loved one that they might never have heard before, and they'll come to know this person in a whole new way.

It's your opportunity to bring a smile to the sad person's face as you recite a joke the deceased always told. It's your moment to heal a wound with kindness. It's your gift to reincarnate that deceased person and see them come alive again, just for a while, as you think back to all they did for those they loved. A condolence card with your personal thoughts is a poignant way to share with the family how much the lost one meant to everyone. The card may be kept on their fireplace mantle for months, reminding them someone else cared and took the time to let them know.

After you complete the condolence card, you will feel better about yourself. Pat yourself on the back for being a good person, for showing what some might say is God's love, and for ministering to the desolate. When and if *you* lose someone close to you and glance at the thoughtful sympathy cards from friends on your counter, you'll understand why a physical reminder and a story about your family member or friend can mean so much. ●

Chapter Ten

Why I Love Typewriters

"I got your letter," the man purred in his gorgeous Hungarian accent. "I've been circumnavigating the world, and this dates back to May, so I apologize—but it looks … is it typed?"

I hear "Is it typed?" a lot. Older people inspect the watermark and run damp fingers over the words to smudge the ink. A typed letter is an oddity. Most folks haven't received one in years, if ever.

I smiled to myself because I knew I had him. Sexy-voice Man was a donor I had written eight months ago.

There are very few other ways to reach someone that will stay on a desk that long. My objective in typing a letter to someone I'm trying to make a good impression on is to set myself apart. I aim to give them something that stays on their desk and makes them remember me every time they look at it. Think about it—how can *you* set yourself apart?

While I ultimately didn't get the big bucks from this donor, I considered it a win because the letter proved to open the door to a person I had been chasing for a long time. He was now a contact that went beyond just elusive. He was officially a connection I could call on.

I am not an artist like my daughter or a major television producer like my husband, but I do one thing well: I type letters people keep and *remember.* The art of letter writing to make an impact or leave an impression is the grown-up version of wooing the pen pal in junior high—with far more lucrative results! If I send a message I've taken the time to type, the recipient will appreciate my care, and hopefully that will make them feel positive to my cause. I also can bet with about 99 percent accuracy that my typed snail mail letter is the only one they've received that week, month, or year.

I type super-fast, about 110 words a minute, which makes the process zen-like because I'm not aware of my body. I'm a robot whose hands take on a rhythm of their own. The average typing speed is about sixty words a minute, so I'm significantly faster. When I'm on the keyboard, the more rapidly my fingers go, the calmer I feel. The fastest typist in the world, Stella Pajunas, had a peak speed of 216 words a minute (in 1946 on an IBM Selectric typewriter).[32] I wish I could have seen her play her instrument in person, and I'm grateful there is a black-and-white film clip on YouTube of Miss Pajunas achieving over 140 words per minute for an entire hour.

Like her, I approach my machine with a sense of calm and let my fingers hover over the keyboard, not thinking about it too much. My morning routine after coffee is to send a newspaper clipping with a typed note, a birthday horoscope, or a real letter. The last thing I do at night is create my to-do list for the next day. Sitting in the near dark, hammering away on my favorite Olympia Electronic Compact 2, I empty my brain so that I can sleep.

I've been a typewriter devotee since age thirteen—and even earlier, if you count my fascination with my mother's green Olympia.

Coaster holder gifted to Erica by Steve and Carol Gerard.

My feet couldn't touch the floor when I sat in front of it. (See picture on page 15.)

Typewriters served as a huge confidence builder for me when I first began writing. They allowed me relative anonymity to reach out to folks and not feel judged as I might in a one-on-one conversation. They gave me a voice. They helped me calm down and focus. They improved my productivity and brought in extra income via secretarial work or typing papers for friends. They got me summer jobs and helped me save for college. They gave me an edge when I was hiring people for television production because I could type as fast as a candidate's former boss could talk, so I would record three references instead of two—and guarantee the candidate would be fully vetted by the time I hired them. Typewriters made me happy and secure in whatever position I held, as if I were bringing my best friend along to work.

I don't expect you to become an instant fan. If you're easily frustrated at learning a new skill late in life, it can be frustrating to learn where to place your fingers. As in learning how to play the piano, you have to practice. Once you get a little speed going, though, it's a whole different experience. There's that "hundred-hour rule": It takes a hundred hours of deliberate practice to go from zero skill to being better than 95 percent of the population. You may adapt faster if you're already good on a phone keyboard. If you notice, your phone also has the "QWERTY" setup, only with the numbers accessible on another screen. The two-finger hunt and peck you use won't work for a typewriter keyboard, though, so you'll have to wrap your brain around another approach.

I've counseled many parents with fidgety children to consider having them try out a typewriter. The banging away aspect of it is fun, for one thing. It's powerful acoustics to hit a key and hear a sound, and if your typewriter has a bell when you pull the carriage across, so much the better. If the child has messy printing (let's not even consider their handwriting legibility anymore), a neatly typed paper will impress their teacher. Of course, they can use their regular laptop and print it out that way, but this "new" approach will set them apart.

I once saw a feature story on the local news in Mesa, Arizona, about teenager Mark Johnson who hauled his grandpa's old 1964 Smith Corona to school; it was so popular the administration was thinking of adding typewriter classes to the curriculum. Mark, who has ADHD, pointed out there were no distractions, no AI prompts: "It's just you and the keys. What you said (in the letter) is what you said, and nothing can change that."

A typewriter is also a good conversation starter. I used my mother's typewriter to lure Arthur Rubin, our fourth-grade class's math genius, to look at the Greek symbols on her machine. I was the only girl he invited to his birthday party, so I know he was impressed.

A warning: Typewriter love is contagious. My brother-in-law Gary McKee caught the bug and tracked down an ultraportable three-inch-tall Corona Zephyr, vintage 1938. His parking lot transaction went for $50 and was a great score. It cost more than that to get it working smoothly, but Gary was still stoked.

Another purchase: Director of Photography Ted Ashton felt aggrieved when he couldn't stop a semitruck loaded with machines being trashed at ABC network's studio offices. Years later, he's rescuing odd castoffs from antique shops and getting them fixed. If you become inspired, there are typewriter mechanics and collectors around the world. Shops are scarce—around 250 exist in the U.S. For example, Manhattan, New York, once had hundreds; now there are three. If you live in Los Angeles, I'll happily meet you at Rees Electronics in Westwood and introduce you to my "mechanic," Mr. Helmut Schulze. Just as my husband has car mechanics he relies on, I couldn't exist without Mr. Schulze.

Vintage typewriters are making a comeback, and like vinyl records and turntables, Millennials love this throwback to a simpler time. Boomers are already aware of typewriters, although it's unusual to use one on a regular basis now. Sixteen-year-old Gen Z girls are into them, too, and machines painted bright "Barbie pink" get snapped up immediately. I worry about how we'll find and train the next generation of repair people—but this is the kind of thing that keeps *me* up at night, so don't you fret about it.

How Can You Learn How to Type?

If you get the bug and want to start typing, online apps, such as Monkeytype and TypingClub, can help you learn finger placement, exercises, and repetitions to get comfortable with the keyboard. It takes practice, so hang in there. Touch typing is based on the notion that each finger has its own area on the keyboard. Thanks to that setup, you can type without looking at the keys. Your fingers will develop "muscle memory" and remember where to go. (I joke with my trainer that my leg muscles have "amnesia" when I haven't worked out in a while, but my fingers never do!)

I haven't used either of them, but they look simple enough, and it's way more fun to practice in your own setting instead of squirming at a hard plastic desk with a strict junior high school teacher watching you "hunt and peck" and counting your mistakes!

Typewriting as Art

If it's typed, it's art. Each page is one of a kind, and errors or the "XXXs" used to cover the wrong characters make it delightful. Imagine the author streaming the words from their consciousness, letting it all fly out—therapy at its simplest. (There are métiers called "Typewriter Art" and "Concrete Poetry." Both use a typewriter to "draw" a picture. Recall the so-called Typewriter Artist, Paul Smith, mentioned earlier.)

I've appreciated typewriters more since I've started cranking out so much correspondence. My friends bestow all things "ASDF" (the first four letters on the middle line of the keyboard) on me: tiny metal replicas, coasters, a box created from discarded letter keys, colorful paintings, black-and-white wall art, warm flannel blankets, a vintage pink eraser with a brush on the other end to clean up mistakes, and special erasable paper used before the invention of Wite-Out. (You could do what actor Tom Hanks, an avid collector of typewriters, does: Put "XXX" over the goof and keep going.) If you're using a newer model machine and make a mistake, smear an opaque white correction fluid over it; once that is dry, you can type or handwrite over it.

I once wrote a thank you note to a crew member from my husband Vin's television show production for his courtesy when I visited the set, and he confessed he was so moved by my note that he unearthed a long-forgotten typewriter stashed in his closet. The ribbon was dry as dust, so he hand-inked the cloth *letter by letter*. I was super impressed. I'd never considered hand-inking; this was very, very cool. Now our bond is in permanent black ink.

Update: Ted Ashton (mentioned previously) bought two more typewriters from thrift shops in Arizona. He now has four machines. He's caught the fever!

I received a lovely testimonial from Samantha Weaver, M.S. CCC-SLIP, Director, Academy of Orofacial Myofunctional Therapy (Los Angeles), who said:

> *A few years ago, I was on the phone with my mother who reminded me of all the wonderful letters I used to write her when I was living abroad. I loved hearing that she had kept them all in a drawer and I wondered what it would be like to read those letters I had written as a nineteen-year-old girl. That got me thinking a lot about the practice of letter writing, and how this lost art was an ache in my soul I felt compelled to rekindle.*

Somewhat fortuitously, I met Erica not long after this. We were both at a friend's party, where the theme was to make crafts out of an old wedding dress. Erica sat at her station with a typewriter nearly as elegant as she was, and offered to type phrases of our choice on heavy cream-colored Crane letter paper to create our own stationery. She was like a letter Fairy Godmother who fluttered into my life to revive this beautiful practice!

Within a few weeks I went with Erica to visit Mr. Schulze's typewriter store in Westwood, Los Angeles—another gem of a long-lost era institution. Inside, typewriters are literally stacked to the ceiling! Every kind of typewriter is there to look at and feel. Mr. Schulze took a lot of time with me, to help me find "the one." I knew the minute I felt the weight of the keys on a 1977 gray-blue Adler with a matching blue cord, I had found my baby!

I cannot say enough about getting back to the practice of letter writing and using a typewriter to write these notes. I use my Adler to do my morning pages and feel like this practice is both poetic and tangible. Plus it's fun and seeing my "baby" on my desk inspires me every time I lay eyes on her to insert paper and begin clacking.

I've had other people get inspired, track down a typewriter, and then send me their results. One such story is from Jerri Churchill, Stage Manager for Vin's television show *America's Funniest Videos*. After a company party Vin and I threw for his staff, I wrote Jerri and her family a Thank You for a beach-scented candle she gave us. After receiving my letter, she was inspired to start upping her own responses— and to my surprise, she bought herself an IBM typewriter (for the great price of $100). She

declared the three-paragraph technique was life-changing. Her feedback always reminds me that sharing the joy of writing a Thank You is my purpose.

Another Jerry—Hallanger—also loves these machines.

My fondness for typing and typewriters began at an early age. I always loved the sound of the typewriter. The clack, clack, clack was like music to my ears. I was a huge fan of Ernest Hemingway. I saw photographs of him sitting at his typewriter. When I was in my sophomore year of high school, I took a typing class. I was the only boy in the class. All of my classmates were girls. When we were given typing assignments in class, I was always the last one to finish typing. The teacher did not seem amused. However, I learned to type and that was my goal. After I completed the class, there was no more hunting and pecking on the typewriter. I have had at least one typewriter in my possession since I was 15 years old. I am especially fond of vintage portable typewriters. I did however, have an IBM Selectric. That was the Rolls Royce of typewriters as far as I was concerned.

I now have 9 portable manual typewriters. They range in age from the 1930's to the 1970's. One of my favorites is the Olivetti Lettera 22. It's the same model that Francis Ford Coppola wrote the screenplay for "The Godfather" on.

Typewriters have been a huge part of my life. I type all of my personal correspondence on a typewriter.

Fondly,
Jerry

Jerri Churchill

Ms. Erica Di Bona

Dear Erica,

When I Opened the beautiful typewriter blanket you sent me, I couldn't believe what I was seeing! Is it possible that there are more people on this planet other than just you and I that are OBSESSED with typewriters?! Apparently so! It took no time at all to decide where I would display it. It is hanging right over the back of my sectional couch that sits next to my typing area in m yfamily room. The colors are just perfect for my home! I have also really enjoyed reading the articles you sent me. Thank you so much for your thoughtfulness, Erica.

Last week, Winston came to my little slice of heaven, Rees Electronics Typewriter Repair Shop. I introduced him to two men who have now become my friends: Mr. Helmut Schulze and Mr. Steve Pine. They were happy to meet Winston Churchill! Ha! Mr. Schulze overheard Winston and I talking about "Erica" and his face lit up. "You know Erica?!", he exclaimed. I guess you are quite famous in the world of typewriters! Ha!

Would you believe I bought another typewriter?! It is another IBM Correcting Selectric II but a smaller model. Only 15% of these are the small model. I bought it for my office in our Arizona home. I realized I never want to be without a typewriter!

I have so many things I want to tell you about when I next see you. I can not wait to tell you about all of the wonderful responses I have received about the typewritten letters I have sent. All because of you, Erica! I would welcome the chance to do any proofreading on your typewriter book if that would be helpful to you. Thank you so much again for your kindness.

Warm regards,

Jerri
Jerri

Testimonial from
Jerri Churchill, new
typewriter lover.

Buyer Beware

Helpful Hints to Find the Right Machine

By now you may be thinking, "I wonder if I should buy my own typewriter?" What's involved in that? What should you know before the quest? I asked my friend Pamela Rogow, owner of WPM Typewriter Shop[33] in Philadelphia, Pennsylvania, what she tells her customers. It turns out she has a series of questions she directs them to consider before they choose a machine.

What Kind of Machine Do You Want?

Do you want a desktop or portable? Desktop is a typewriter that will live in one place on your desk. It's heavy—usually thirty-five pounds or, in the case of an IBM Selectric, as bulky as forty-eight pounds! A portable comes in a hard case that protects the machine as you carry it around with you.

Most people are interested in nimble, smaller portable typewriters because they have portable lives and less space. (They may also be used to using a mini iPad.) Disclaimer: If you want to purchase a desktop machine, this section won't help you much.

Considering a Portable?

Do you prefer manual or electric? You need finger strength to punch the keys on a manual, whereas an electric may be slightly easier and faster to type on.

- How old-school do you want to go?
- Do you have enough experience using one already, or should you test them both?
- Are you able to lug around a heavier one? What does it weigh?

How Will It Feel?

- What is the sensory experience of striking the keys and returning the carriage?
- Is it satisfying? Does it have the right tension and speed? Are the keys the right distance from each other? Does this experience feel the most comfortable to you?
- Buyer beware: If you're buying a typewriter online, you won't be able to try typing because you're not exactly there in person.

Some typewriter shops don't let you try out the typewriter. And not all stores are the same; some have different versions of the same model. One store could also charge triple the rate, so check prices online.

Sturdiness and Size

Some typewriters are sturdy, and some are more lightweight. In the seventies and eighties, typewriter companies introduced ultra-portables, which had slim profiles and were often made of plastic. Ultra-portable typewriters include those from Olympia, Adler Tippa, and Royal Royalite.

Design

- How much do you care about the decorative, nostalgic, and historic aspects of your typewriter?
- Do you want one that looks like your grandfather's? Will it go with your office space or bedroom décor?
- What color do you want? (Pink is a premium color—expect an upcharge at many stores.)

Typeface

- Do you like the typeface (font)?
- Is it appropriate for your use?
- There are basically two sizes of font with different looks for both alphabet and numbers: Pica and Elite. There are also specialized typefaces, of which favorites include Cursive and Sans Serif.

Price

A lower-cost machine (say below $245) may be fussier. There may be some dings or scratches, so it won't be cosmetically perfect. The machine may have a little glitch, such as the tab not working—but if it's for kids, they don't like using tabs anyway. Despite these idiosyncratic problems the machine itself may work fine. Think of it like buying a used car.

To do a price comparison, you can look at the eBay completed sales or check with Facebook's "Antique Typewriter Collector's Group." People post a listing for typewriters they're thinking of getting and ask the group how much they should pay and whether it's a good deal.

Scott Apostolou, a collector friend, says the price "depends on what level you're shopping on and how patient/lucky you are. For example, buying a fifties-era Smith Corona Silent Super at the Los Altos, California, store would probably be between $400 and $500. EBay ranges from low to high $100s. I found one on Craigslist in Portland that wasn't the sexiest version of it but really in excellent condition and a dream to type on for $33. Etsy for that model might be high $200s and up."

Features

- Does your typewriter have a tab key, a tab maker, or a column maker? Some don't.
- Is your typewriter self-correcting? Most don't have the feature.
- Does your typewriter have a spool ribbon?
- With manual typewriters, you may have a power space bar. You press it down hard, and it "zip zip zips" continuously.
- Are there continuous keys? Usually these are period keys, and on some machines, they function as the hyphen/underscore.

Ribbons

Ink ribbons are easy to find and inexpensive. Back when typewriters were used in offices, every secretary in America could thread a spooled ribbon, and so can you!

You have an option of either a red-and-black ribbon or just a black ribbon. Do you care? FYI, the red-and-black combo doesn't last as long; a black ribbon will last around six months. If

Typewriter type cleaner from Erica's collection (gift from Heidi Farkash).

you have a red ribbon, red always goes on the bottom. I've had a navy blue ribbon and a brown one (but it didn't show up all that well). In the end, the classic red-and-black combo is easiest to find, and I'm not sure the "surprise" element of brown or blue blew away anybody but me. I did order matching stationery for each color to make it have a coordinated look, and that gave me a frisson of excitement.

- Big-box stores (such as Staples Office Supply) now sell typewriter spools, and some are reported to have better quality than others.
- Some typewriters, usually modern electric brands, use hard plastic cartridges instead of ribbons. My Olympia Electronic Compact 2 does, and I'm eternally grateful because it keeps my fingers from getting smudged when I change it.

Purchasing Typewriters

- Once you've found a machine you like, does the typewriter store offer a warranty for service and parts? Some places might have weird exceptions. Is there a warranty or return policy?
- If you buy at an antique store, it is sold "as is." You are buying it in whatever condition it's in, "with all faults." The seller is not required to fix anything if they say "as is." What you see (or don't see) is what you get.
- Bring your own paper if you want to try it out. Mr. Helmut Schulze, my mechanic, explained that older machines like two pieces of paper instead of one to protect the carriage. I've not really adopted this approach, but it seems like a good habit if you commit.

Buying Online

- If you buy the typewriter online, it will need a new ribbon. Often a seller will say, "We didn't test it with a ribbon." How do you know it works? You don't!

- Look to make sure you're not buying a foreign keyboard by accident. Buy one with an American QWERTY keyboard.
- Check to see whether it has specialized keys for accounting, foreign languages, or chemical symbols or whether it's "bare bones."
- Does it have a hard traveling case?

Shipping

Make sure they know how to properly ship the machine to you. Many typewriters have been killed by improper shipping. Typewriters are actually quite fragile and delicate. Pretend you're wrapping an Egyptian mummy. The machine itself should be wrapped in medium-size bubble wrap inside the case. Large-size bubble wrap should be used to protect the entire thing. Styrofoam peanuts or wadded-up newspaper should fill the empty part of the box. If you're a musician who has ever tried to send a precious instrument somewhere, you understand what I'm saying.

Overall, it's better to go and pick it up in person if you can.

I'm not saying you need to use a typewriter to begin writing your Thank You notes—do whatever charms you and brings you to your desk to communicate your gratitude. As my father used to say, "Life is about keeping yourself entertained."

If you'd rather bake a loaf of banana bread or send flowers or chocolates to thank someone, go for it. If your child loves folding paper airplanes, have him scrawl a message on the wing. Paint a rock. Be creative.

Whatever would make you happy will make the recipient happy too. And isn't that what we're after, when it's all said and done? Letters and thank yous have no expiration date. You will continue to see them open doors, leading you to new and deeper friendships and unexpected happiness and connection. Be grateful for the gift of the Thank You! ●

May 21, 2024

Dear Friends:

You don't have to do it my way. Yuo don't need to
buy a typewriter, or type it on your printer. You
don't have to tell a mini-story, or write it
diary-style, or knock yourself out.

It shouldn't be something you dread, like when you
were little and your Mom was standing over you.

It should return major rewards, if you take a
few moments to let someone know they helped you
out when they gave you the job, or the gift they
sent added to your happiness, or they're important
in your life.

You may be surprised at how good writing
makes you feel.
Perhaps you'll get a response back.
Maybe you'll start to check your mailbox and
see what tumbles out.

If you start a connection through correspondence,
give yourself credit for deepening the
relationship.
You touched someone's heart.
You sent out some love in what can be an uncaring
place.
In the act of letter-writing, you made the
world a friendlier place.

Keep going. See where it takes you. And
remember "A letter is better".

Love, *Erica Gerard Di Bona*
Erica Gerard Di Bona

A final letter to you,
the Reader.

A typical day of Erica's outgoing mail.

Letter by Letter:
The Making of This Book and Its Many Thank Yous

It all began in my memoir writing class when my teacher, **Linda Schreyer**, suggested I start keeping copies of thank you letters I'd sent. Linda confessed that she gathers all my correspondence in an "Erica file" and said I have a special gift I should showcase. My fellow writers **Darlene Basch** and Mimi Starrett agreed, and an idea was born. These letters were different, too, since they were all typed on a typewriter. When we merged with the rest of the Ojai Women's Writers Group, **Dr. Paula Bernstein, Cathy Novak, Laurie Collister**, and **Hyla Cohn** also urged me to "go for it."

The first iteration was "recipe style," with a letter on one side of the page and a response on the other—more intimate than instructional. Then, through a divine Facebook introduction, I met best-selling author and manifestation teacher **Jennifer Blanchard**. A developmental editor, she assigned me deadlines, helped me construct a book outline, and provided feedback and emotional support.

Now this project felt like something. I just needed someone to sit in the room with me and help me get a real draft together. **Dean Katharyne Mitchell** from the University of California, Santa Cruz introduced me to her daughter, the always-positive **Sage Mitchell-Sparke**. Sage taught writing to other students at her alma mater, Oberlin College. She is the only person I've ever known who can read a hardback book on the bouncy city bus. We shared countless hours crafting this tome. Sage was my first editor, cheerleader, and co-conspirator.

When we felt we had a viable book, we interfaced with **Steve Harrison**'s Get Published Now marketing group. **Deb Englander** was especially helpful.

After I made a thirty-five-second pitch to twelve agents, **Lisa Hagan** of Lisa Hagan Literary took me on. Lisa loved the book's thank you message and worked hard to sell it, but nothing congealed, and we parted ways with no hard feelings.

Another delay.

Sage moved to England for grad school. The project sat dormant. Acquaintances who hadn't seen me in a while would inquire, "How's the book?" I'd shrink—it was embarrassing to admit I *still* wasn't done.

The truth was, after the lack of interest from publishers, I didn't have the heart to start again. But others still believed in this book—and in me.

Support came from "typewriter friends." My typewriter mechanic, **Mr. Helmut Schulze**, was enthusiastic about my project. He knows I generate a thousand typed letters a year since he fixes my well-used machines. (I have multiple, including a Smith-Corona manual he painted silver and gold, featured on the cover.)

There's a "Typosphere" out there for those of us who love ASDF. My first mechanic, **Ermanno Marzorati**, insisted I meet **Louise A. Marler**. He knew we'd get along—she's a Typewriter Artist. Louise revealed her dream of submitting a machine from her family's St. Louis, Missouri repair store to the Smithsonian.

Vin and I talked to **John Gray**, Director of the National Museum of American History, and brokered a deal for actor/typewriter collector **Tom Hanks** to place a couple of his beloved machines in the museum and for **Steve Soboroff** to do so as well. (Steve recently donated much of his collection to the museum.)

My friend **Larry Rogow** also did some matchmaking. "You should meet my sister," he said, and he was right. **Pamela Rogow**, who founded W.P.M. Typewriter Shop in Philadelphia, has since schooled me on everything from equipment to philosophy. We "kick the tires" and chat about our beloved IBM Selectrics, Olympias, Royals, Hermes 3000s, and more.

Elderly machines need love and attention. **Pedro Hernandez**, my other mechanic, cheerfully comes to my house when the ball of my IBM Selectric is frozen. He was one of the few people who entered the house all masked up during COVID-19; he was an "essential worker" in my mind! He always scolds, "You type too fast—you beat the machine." I tell him I'm *never* going to slow down. (I type 110 words a minute.) We both laugh.

Also in my community: **Scott Apostolou**, who lovingly oversaw getting my ailing mother's loden green Olympia (and the one I learned on) fixed, although it was already a struggle for her to walk down the hall to her desk. Scott once set out every single machine he owned so that I could admire the differences among the keyboards. His excellent advice on how to choose a machine is included in this book. His wife, **Christy Hale**, is a prolific children's book writer and has been my friend since seventh grade.

Karen Schmidt, my college roommate who worked at the Getty Museum in Publications for decades, also encouraged me. She braved a shady parking lot deal to buy me a sleek, portable Olympia with one red return key for my birthday. We attend the Printers Fair each year and geek out about all things printing press and papyrus. When I was choosing the best cover (and making other decisions) for this book, I knew Karen would give me sage advice—and she did, just as she always does.

Gloria Shepard and **Gloria Gordon**, who met in their late eighties at a grieving group (and ditched it for a singing class instead), exchanged handwritten letters on a regular basis and were my first proofreaders. We shared a love for Forever 21, which is sadly also gone. I wish they could have seen this book.

Dr. Sarosh Motivala, my psychologist, got me unstuck at various points in my trajectory. He helped me create a blog called *The Art of Thank You*, find a new profession as a "friend-raiser" in Development, and kept me moving toward completing this book. His lovely mother, **Roshan Motivala**, is my newest pen pal.

Various other professionals also educated me. **Marleah Leslie**, a major publicist in Hollywood, kindly offered her experience on how to craft my message and promote the book. She's married to my ex-husband, **Josh Goldstein**. Their son **Justin Goldstein**, still in junior high school at the time, researched hashtags, similar blogs, and social media influencers for me so that I'd understand the competition.

Gary H. Grossman, a television producer and author of international political thrillers with whom Vin collaborated on his autobiography, crafted an entire prototype—bound and illustrated—as to how I could rewrite the book. He helped me imagine what its final form could be.

James Goldin, a writer and TV producer, gave me a detailed description of what's involved in self-publishing and translated the confusing requirements into English. He also carted a typewriter to Mr. Schulze so that his UC Santa Cruz graduate Charles could write on it.

Justin DiPego, a self-published author and UC Santa Cruz alum, gifted me a copy of his own novel and gave me the skinny on the "Big Five" publishing companies (i.e., HarperCollins, Simon & Schuster, Macmillan, Hachette, and Penguin Random House).

SQuire Rushnell and **Louise DuArt**, who cowrote the inspiring and uplifting *The Godwink Series*, motivated me many times to keep believing in myself. They were ready to share their connections, and for that, I owe them a big "Thank You."

Painter **Marisa Murrow** shares how she keeps herself inspired to create, and her lively flower paintings hang above my desk. She adds beauty to life through her love of art and nature. I consider her my creative muse: Whenever I was ready to give up, I'd get a note or handmade card from Marisa reminding me to stay the course.

World-renowned potter **Adam Silverman** and I collect hotel stationery, especially if it's embossed with our names when we're a guest. Adam has always coveted his personalized Chateau Marmont paper—and once mourned his dwindling supply. I leaped into action and begged the hotel General Manager to get him more. Since then, Adam's sent missives from Japanese hotels; I've returned responses on fancy pads from Emirates Airlines. It's getting hard to top ourselves, though! Hotels don't carry preprinted paper like that anymore, and a yellow Post-it doesn't suffice as a place to write a heartfelt note. I take my own notepads to hotels so that I can thank the staff.

Since I send out so many clippings, packages, and letters, I once relied on **Tim Shackelford**, my knight in shining armor from the U.S. Postal Service, to lug in incoming mail and take mine out. When he retired, I was devastated. We had a goodbye dinner. He was always a bright spot in my day.

The march to completion continued. When I confided in my trainer, **Malin Svensson**, that I was done with the first draft of this book and had stalled out, she suggested I contact **Kimberly O'Hara**—a writing coach Malin had worked with to produce her *own* book, about fitness.

Kim recognized that this was a combination of memoir and "how-to" but needed to be reworked. She and I forged a way to save most of what I'd written, deleted some memoir content, and added more how-to. I decided to self-publish. Then, things heated up.

Kim turned me onto **Fabi Preslar**, founder and president of SPARK Publications. Along with several of her talented SPARKlers, she has helped design, produce, and publish my beautiful book. Special thanks to Creative Director **Larry Preslar**, Production Manager **Jaclyn**, and Special Projects Coordinator **Sofi.** I joked that Larry "sees me" because I could describe a vague idea and he would translate that into a layout more eye-catching than anything I could have ever imagined.

Melissa Crandall, who worked with **Linda Schreyer** years ago, stepped in to support me on version #2. She unflinchingly took on gnarly assignments that gave me a headache just thinking about them. She meticulously crafted all the footnotes; uploaded the pictures, graphics, and script to the design company; and understood what Fabi Preslar needed for information sharing. She's an ace proofreader and always remembers what's where. Without her, this book would never have come together. I have notes all over the place to "Ask Melissa."

All along the way, kind people encouraged me. **Helen Hintz**, a Smithsonian Institution board member, flew into Washington, D.C., to attend a class I taught about Thank You notes to eighteen museum directors. We both love the U.S. Postal Service.

Christine Udvar-Hazy, whose family founded the Smithsonian Institution's National Air and Space Museum and began the Smithsonian Regional Council program, is a kindred spirit in believing there's power in gracious correspondence.

Kevin L. Beggs, Chair/Chief Creative Officer of Lionsgate Television, was criss-crossing the United States on business when I asked him if he could write a testimonial. He crafted an extraordinary letter that is the foreword to this book.

Donelle Dadigan, founder of the Hollywood Museum (and member of the Smithsonian National Board), offered to host a book-signing party in the lobby of her museum when everything was all said and done. We both have the same red-and-white Kate Spade "typewriter" purses and have fun showcasing them at the same events.

Franklin Levy, Esq., aka Biff, and **Lynda Levy** edited and commented on one draft of the book between them. Lynda also created an original art piece for me—a typewriter with a piece of paper in the carriage that says, "Dear Erica, Thank you for trying to make the world a kinder place with your Thank You notes. Don't give up."

Annie Sprinkle and **Dr. Beth Stephens**, who teach in the Arts Division at the University of California, Santa Cruz, sent me books about how to greenlight your project—and Annie had a brainstorm one weekend and introduced me to a graphic designer she hoped could help me get it all together. (Annie and Beth are well-regarded "ecosexuals" and "married to the Earth.")

Jerry Hallanger, another typewriter aficionado (guess by which method we correspond!), shares war stories even though we've never met.

Samantha Weaver, whom I met at a party at **Steve** and the late **Licia Paskay**'s house, had me speak to her Academy of Orofacial Myofunctional Therapy community about building a business with letter writing. I introduced her to Mr. Schulze; she trotted home with a beautiful blue typewriter and a blue cord.

Brian Corbell, whose typing skills saved him from the front lines because he was the only young man who could handle an office job in World War II, gifted me his beautiful machine.

Ian L. Brooks, my real estate guru / photographer / Renaissance man, eased the pain of my sixty-fifth birthday with his ego-boosting compliments, a designer purse, and a sleek portable Olivetti Underwood Lettera 33 featuring one red key.

Amy Green, who spots extra-special stationery and notepads, used a stylus to cut an image of a typewriter without breaking the paper once—and hand-carried it to Los Angeles from Providence, Rhode Island. She sourced an original piece by Typewriter Artist **James Cook** called *Typewriter Typing a Typewriter*. It's amazing but copyrighted, so look it up online.

Michael Seales, principal engineer at Riot Games, Inc., which develops video games and esports tournaments (*League of Legends*), explained corporate culture for companies like his, where a formal "Thank You" note doesn't add much weight to hiring decisions because interviews are outsourced to a recruiting company—and tech guys don't use paper!

However, **Robert W. Glass**, executive vice president of corporate development for the Robert Half International staffing agency, reassured me his firm still counts a Thank You note very highly when they decide who to hire.

Other folks whose correspondence graces my mailbox include my pen pals, ranging from ages four to one hundred: **Rio Lucas**, who began writing me letters in nursery school and who is now in high school. **Taj Britton**, who became my weekly pandemic correspondent when he was in elementary school and made those two years more bearable. **Cate Ferrall**, my pen pal from age three to college who wanted a typewriter for her sixteenth birthday (I directed her to W.P.M. Typewriter Shop in Philadelphia, where my friend **Pamela Rogow** helped her choose a British beauty). And **Doris Nemtzow**, who is still cranking out handwritten letters on lined floral paper at age one hundred. The incredible gold-dipped typewriter key necklace I have is a gift from Doris, who originally had it made for herself.

Donna Brown Guillaume, whom I met at my first television job out of college, has sent me more cards than anyone else. (We joke about making a "dysfunctional family greeting card" line but haven't done it yet.)

And, last but not least, my everlasting gratitude goes out to my family.

Vin Di Bona, my patient husband, who never complains when he sees my office light on late at night or hears my typewriter clackety-clacking. He also benefits from the fact that, after we attend a party, I'll write the Thank You the next day and he gets the credit. He sends his own gracious letters to *America's Funniest Videos* staff and understands how special it is to receive such a missive from the boss. A sentimental man, he's a stickler for wanting a holiday card sent through the mail, not just handed to him.

Jamie Goldstein, my daughter, who claims she doesn't enjoy generating Thank You notes but does a beautiful job. Her artistic genius is the *true* talent in the family. She makes sure I don't look too "matchy-matchy" or misuse slang, and she always fact-checks my sources.

My sister **Annie Gerard**, who's the smarter of us two, quicker on the uptake with technology, and a master chef. Her husband, **Gary McKee**, surprised me once when he sent a typed note—on his own newly acquired typewriter. An aerospace engineer, he invented a "cordless electric" and joined the cult of typewriter lovers.

My brother—technical recruiter by day and rock 'n' roll singer by night—**Steven Gerard**, and his wife, **Carol**, who find the most unusual typewriter objects ever.

My mother, **Betty Gerard**, and my father, **Gary Gerard**, who emboldened me as a first-grader to send a Thank You note to President John F. Kennedy for saving us from the Cuban Missile Crisis. Both excellent writers and editors, they would have been delighted to realize that my envelope to the White House ignited a lifelong habit of gratitude expressed through letters.

And, finally, my **Granddaddy Al**, who started it all. I love you and thank you. ●

Thank You! With Love,

Erica

Novelty typewriter
ring holder from
Erica's collection.

Sources

Center for Compassion and Altruism Research and Education, Stanford University Medicine, https://ccare.stanford.edu/research/.

Emmons, R. A. *The Little Book of Gratitude: Create a Life of Happiness and Well-Being By Giving Thanks*. Gaia, 2016. https://psychology.ucdavis.edu/people/raemmons.

Forster, Daniel E., Eric J. Pedersen, Adam Smith, Michael E. McCullough, and Debra Lieberman. "Benefit valuation predicts gratitude." *Evolution and Human Behavior* 38 (2017): 18–26. http://local.psy.miami.edu/faculty/mmccullough/Papers/2017-BenefitValuationPredictsGratitude.pdf.

Froh, Jeffrey J., Todd B. Kashdan, Kathleen M. Ozimkowski, and Norman Miller. "Who benefits the most from a gratitude intervention in children and adolescents? Examining positive affect as a moderator," *Journal of Positive Psychology* 4, no. 5 (2009): 408–422.

Hamadey, Gina. "How to Write a Gratitude Letter." *New York Times*, February 27, 2021. https://www.nytimes.com/2021/02/27/at-home/how-to-write-a-gratitude-letter.html.

Harvard Health Publishing. "Giving thanks can make you happier." Last modified August 14, 2021. https://www.health.harvard.edu/healthbeat/giving-thanks-can-make-you-happier.

Kesarovska, Lydia. "5 Secrets to Having a Give and Take Relationship in 2020." Let's Reach Success. Last modified November 13, 2024. https://letsreachsuccess.com/give-and-take-relationship/.

Kho, Nancy Davis. *The Thank-You Project: Cultivating Happiness One Letter of Gratitude at a Time.* Running Press, 2019.

Rancaño, Vanessa. "Be Kind, Unwind: How Helping Others Can Help Keep Stress In Check." NPR. Last modified December 17, 2015. https://www.npr.org/sections/health-shots/2015/12/17/460030338/be-kind-unwind-how-helping-others-can-help-keep-stress-in-check.

Raposa, Elizabeth B., Holly B. Laws, and Emily B. Ansell. "Prosocial Behavior Mitigates the Negative Effects of Stress in Everyday Life," *Clinical Psychological Science* 4, no. 4 (2016): 691–698. https://journals.sagepub.com/doi/abs/10.1177/2167702615611073.

Seligman, Martin. "The New Era of Positive Psychology." TED Talk, July 21, 2008. Video, 23 min., 42 sec. https://www.ted.com/talks/martin_seligman_the_new_era_of_positive_psychology?subtitle=en.

Endnotes

1 "The Classic Typewriter Page: Typewriter Fonts," Richard Polt, accessed November 19, 2024, https://site.xavier.edu/polt/typewriters/tw-fonts.html.

2 Jeffrey J. Froh, Todd B. Kashdan, Kathleen M. Ozimkowski, and Norman Miller, "Who benefits the most from a gratitude intervention in children and adolescents? Examining positive affect as a moderator," *Journal of Positive Psychology* 4, no. 5 (2009): 408–422.

3 Jan Tuckwood, "Commentary: Oprah Winfrey and the power of validation," *WRAL News*, January 17, 2018, https://www.wral.com/story/commentary-oprah-winfrey-and-the-power-of-validation/17265810/.

4 "International Pen Friends," IPF, accessed November 19, 2024, https://www.ipfworld.com.

5 Serena Smith, "The number of lonely, single men is on the rise," *Dazed*, August 12, 2022.

6 "Dating by Blaine," Blaine Anderson, accessed November 19, 2024, https://www.datingbyblaine.com/.

7 Dale Carnegie, *How to Win Friends and Influence People* (1936), (Simon & Schuster, 2009). Currently fifty million copies are in print in thirty-eight languages worldwide.

8 Guy Trebay, "The Found Art of Thank-You Notes," *New York Times*, April 4, 2014.

9 Lydia Kesarovska, "5 Secrets to Having a Give and Take Relationship in 2020," Let's Reach Success, last modified January 21, 2020, https://letsreachsuccess.com/give-and-take-relationship/.

10 "Jimmy Fallon is Right: 4 Tips for a Powerful Thank You Note," Caren Merrick, accessed November 19, 2024, https://carenmerrick.com/jimmy-fallon-is-right-4-tips-for-a-powerful-thank-you-note/.

11 Maanvi Singh, "Your Health: If You Feel Thankful, Write it Down. It's Good For Your Health," *NPR*, last modified December 24, 2018, https://www.npr.org/sections/health-shots/2018/12/24/678232331/if-you-feel-thankful-write-it-down-its-good-for-your-health.

12 "The Gratitude Journey," Tom Ziglar, accessed November 20, 2024, https://www.ziglar.com/articles/the-gratitude-journey/.

13 Madhuleena Roy Chowdhury, BA," The Neuroscience of Gratitude and Effects on the Brain," Positive Psychology, last modified April 9, 2019, https://positivepsychology.com/neuroscience-of-gratitude/.

14 Vu Le, "20 new rules regarding handwritten thank-you notes we must all adopt immediately," Nonprofit AF, last modified February 6, 2023, https://nonprofitaf.com/2023/02/20-new-rules-regarding-handwritten-thank-you-notes-we-must-all-adopt-immediately/.

15 Vanessa Rancano, "Be Kind, Unwind: How Helping Others Can Help Keep Stress in Check," *NPR*, December 17, 2015, https://www.npr.org/sections/health-shots/2015/12/17/460030338/be-kind-unwind-how-helping-others-can-help-keep-stress-in-check.

16 "Random acts of kindness," Mental Health Foundation, accessed November 20, 2024, https://www.mentalhealth.org.uk/explore-mental-health/kindness-and-mental-health/random-acts-kindness.

17 Harriet Hunter, "AA: Ten Things to Forgive Ourselves to Freedom," Harriet Hunter, last modified April 7, 2021 https://harriethunter.org/aa-ten-things-to-forgive-ourselves-to-freedom.

18 Millennials are people born from 1981 to 1996. Gen Zers are those born from 1997 to 2012. Younger kids, born since 2010 until the time of this publication, are called Generation Alpha or Gen Alpha; they are the children of Millennials.

19 Katie Hurlew, LCSW, "Teen Sexting: What Parents Need to Know," HealthCentral, last updated March 8, 2021, https://www.psycom.net/teen-sexting.

20 Cursive and Handwriting," My Cursive, accessed November 20, 2024, https://mycursive.com. This is a website that tracks cursive writing requirements nationwide.

21 Judith Orloff, MD, "How the Sandwich Technique Can Transform Your Relationships," *Psychology Today*, July 23, 2018, https://www.psychologytoday.com/us/blog/the-empaths-survival-guide/201807/how-the-sandwich-technique-can-transform-your-relationships.

22 Jessica Liebman, "How to Write a Perfect Thank-You Email After a Job Interview," *Business Insider*, April 5, 2019, https://www.businessinsider.com/how-to-write-thank-you-email-after-job-interview-2019-4.

23 Andrew Seaman, "Should You Send Thank-You Notes After Job Interviews?," LinkedIn, last modified August 29, 2023, https://www.linkedin.com/pulse/should-you-send-thank-you-notes-after-job-interviews-andrew-seaman.

24 Microsoft tells you how at https://create.microsoft.com/en-us/learn/articles/how-to-create-stationery-using-templates.

25 Robin Madell, "10 Mistakes to Avoid With a Job Interview Thank-You Email," *U.S. News & World Report*, March 27, 2023, https://money.usnews.com/money/blogs/outside-voices-careers/slideshows/mistakes-to-avoid-on-a-thank-you-email.

26 Vu Le, *Nonprofit AF*, July 22, 2012, https://nonprofitaf.com/.

27 "Newspaper Data," MANSIMedia, the Print & Digital Advertising Authority, accessed November 20, 2024, https://mansimedia.com/expertise/newspaper-data/.

28 "About NCF," Nantucket Comedy, accessed November 20, 2024, https://nantucketcomedy.com/about/.

29 "Kevin Flynn: Fear of Heights," Kevin Flynn Live, accessed November 20, 2024, https://kevinflynnlive.com/fear-of-heights/.

30 Charles C. Ebbets, Lunch atop a Skyscraper, photo, September 20, 1932, https://en.wikipedia.org/wiki/Lunch_atop_a_Skyscraper.

31 "ThoughtFulls Pop-Open Cards," Compendium, Inc., accessed November 20, 2024, https://shop.live-inspired.com/catalog/category/desk-stationery/stationery/pop-open-cards/.

32 Per Ratatype.com.

33 You can find her at WPMTypewriterShop.com.

Meet Erica!

Erica Gerard Di Bona generates 1,000 letters a year with an impressive speed of 110 words per minute (on a typewriter). She may very well be the United States Postal Service's consumer of the year. A former producer in network news, kids' game shows, The Playboy Channel, and documentaries, she has never let a single opportunity for a professional Thank You slide and has often received letters and messages back from such notables as Connie Chung, Norman Lear, and Henry Winkler.

Currently a fundraising consultant for University of California, Santa Cruz and serving on the Board of Trustees for the Smithsonian Regional Council and formerly the Rhode Island School of Design, her unique letters open doors and attract donors.

People frame Erica's snail mail, and she has left her influence on the power of the Thank You with high school and college students, development executives, realtors, dentists, and grateful grandparents.

Erica is a proud UC Santa Cruz Banana Slug and a graduate of the University of California, Los Angeles. She lives in Los Angeles with her television producer husband, artistic daughter, and seven typewriters.

Stay connected with Erica

facebook.com/ArtofThankYou

Typist110@icloud.com

Instagram @powerof_thankyou

ArtofThankYou7557

To order additional books
ArtofThankYou.com

www.ingramcontent.com/pod-product-compliance
Lightning Source LLC
Chambersburg PA
CBHW041140120626
46547CB00020B/3063